Reading Trout Streams

Reading Trout Streams

AN ORVIS GUIDE

Tom Rosenbauer

Illustrations by James Sulham

Lyons & Burford, *Publishers*

Printed in the United States of America

10 9

Illustrations by James Sulham.

All photographs by the author unless otherwise noted.

Library of Congress Cataloging-in-Publication Data

Rosenbauer, Tom.
Reading trout streams.

Bibliography: p.
Includes index.
1. Trout fishing. 2. Rivers. I. Title.
SH687.R69 1988 799.1′755 87–36212
ISBN 0-941130-78-9 (pbk.)

To Tony Skilton
(1945–1986)

Acknowledgments

We never get to fish as much as we like, and in writing a book like this one there are rivers I'd only fished once, or in some cases had never seen. In order to make *Reading Trout Streams* as broad as possible, I was not shy about asking friends for help on rivers and streams they know intimately. I think I've learned something about reading trout streams from everyone I've ever fished with, beginner and expert alike, but I'd like to offer special thanks to the following people: Hilary Bates, Vern Bressler, Chris Child, Alan DeNicola, David Denies, Rusty Gates, Rex Gerlach, Dave Kumlien, Art Lee, Brian O'Keefe, Leigh Perkins, Bill Reed, Ed Schroeder, Jorge Trucco, and Bob White.

Special thanks to Jim Sulham for the marvelous illustrations and valuable input on how to transform this slippery subject into pen and ink; and to Martin Kalish and his crew at Photographer's Eye for the excellent job of processing and printing all those black-and-whites, even though they hate to do them.

Bob Bachman is one of the greatest thinkers in the world on trout and trout streams, and many of my theories on reading water come from discussions with Bob.

Nick Lyons is too nice to his writers. He should be more of a bear—but his never-ending support and help have encouraged most of today's fly-fishing writers.

My wife, Margot Page, is the best editor and agent anyone could have, but even more valuable are the times she kicks me in the butt when I'm whining about not being able to finish a chapter.

Contents

Foreword

One of the several discrete pleasures of being a book editor is that the process encourages you to read closely and in so doing to learn intimately about worlds you thought you knew well or did not know at all. Editing is close reading.

Pure-bred dogs, the Vietnam War, macramé, a New England sea captain made slave to Arabs in North Africa, books by an Olympic swimmer and a woman pioneer in Canada, cook books, travel books, exercise books, literary parodies—a practicing editor handles that kind of disparate fare, and over the years I have; I've also edited a lot of books for fly fishermen. I've been lucky enough to husband into the world original books or reprints by Sparse Grey Hackle, Doug Swisher and Carl Richards, Lee Wulff, Joan Salvato Wulff, Dave Whitlock, Vince Marinaro, Art Flick, Darrel Martin, Charlie Brooks, Lefty Kreh, Paul Schullery, and a host of others.

Only once before have I written an introduction to a book I edited—though, having seen the texts first, and being an enthusiast before being an editor, I've often wanted to shout out to the world about what I'd found. That's the second of the pleasures you get being an editor: often you're the first person other than the author to see a new book, and a good book is always a portal into another man's mind and into a new world.

In Tom's case, I hesitated to accept his invitation to write this Foreword only because I've written a lot of them lately; but, with unabashed pleasure, I happen to enjoy writing about what I like—and I like what Tom has written very much. Anyway, I'd fished with him on the Willowemoc and had been impressed not only by his deft and authoritative casting but by his sure fish-sense. He knew where the fish were; he wasted little time on dead water.

Fish-sense is an odd quality. In fishermen with weak technical skills, it can mask a lot of incompetence; in the best fishermen, it's lethal. You *must* know where the fish are and this takes years of experience coupled with solid study of the literature of trout biology. Tom brings both to this book. He has been a fisherman since childhood, he has fished all kinds of trout water in all parts of the country, and he's a true student of the best modern research on trout rivers. He knows what questions to ask—and how to answer them.

Why would a trout be precisely here or there in a river? Where will it be in relation to currents of this speed and pockets of that size and pools with this configuration? What are a trout's needs? How do diurnal and seasonal changes affect where a trout will be? When will a trout face *down*stream? How can stream reading be coupled with the problems of approach and presentation—and even etiquette?

Tom has addressed these and scores of similar questions. He has done so thoughtfully, wisely, and always with the practical fly fisherman in mind; best of all, being a gifted teacher he has done that most difficult of tricks: conveyed to others clearly and well what he knows. Not all people in possession of special knowledge can do this. It requires a special gift.

What Tom has done in *Reading Trout Streams* is to take the mysterious forms of current, rock, bank, pool, pocket, and run and make them "readable" to someone who has only vaguely thought of how these factors affect where a trout will be in a river; he has offered the intermediate fly fisherman a firmer grasp of material he knew only slenderly; and he has reminded the advanced fly fisherman of what he knew only instinctively perhaps. All will find valuable insights in this book—and all will appreciate the way in which Tom has made the vibrant life in rivers and streams more understandable.

Reading Trout Streams is a solid contribution to the literature of trout fishing and rivers. In its thoughtful prose and helpful illustrations, you'll find insights that will make you more knowing and confident along rivers. Reading this book closely in the dead of winter, in a grey riverless city, I've found revelations that make me itch to be on the water, where I can use what I've learned fruitfully. I think you will, too.

NICK LYONS
New York City
January 1988

Preface

Reading a trout stream is more than looking at the currents on the surface. A canoeist reads currents, learning to avoid rocks beneath the surface, or predicting how a sharp bend in the river will influence the course of his or her craft. Yet an accomplished canoeist will be only a hair better than the average person in predicting where trout will be found in a stream. To read a stream, you need an understanding of a trout's life history, behavior, and requirements for survival—facets of the world of trout fishing that are easier to learn than fancy knots, less frustrating than ironing out bugs in your casting, and eminently more useful at a cocktail party than entomology.

This book will tell you where to cast a fly but it has other practical applications as well. It will teach you where *not* to cast, where to wade, and where *not* to wade so you don't frighten the fish. You will learn about the places trout favor at different times of the season. It will give you the confidence to predict, with pinpoint accuracy, where a trout is most likely to be lying in almost any stream situation you'll encounter. Why should you care about such precision? Isn't just slapping your fly in the vicinity of a trout good enough? If your fly is the right pattern, won't a fish rush across a pool to grab it? No. Trout have narrow feeding lanes, and will seldom move more than a foot for food. And in tricky drag situations, any help in predicting where the fish will be is a blessing, especially in those spots where you can expect only a few inches of drag-free float.

Skill in reading a stream is essential for success if you're fishing "blind"—that is, fishing to places in the river where trout should be, not to visibly feeding fish. A bad blind cast will spook unseen fish—many more than will see the proper presentation of your fly. And even if you only cast dry flies to rising trout, you need to be able to read a stream. You can't observe the whole pool at once; knowing where trout are likely to be helps you spot the rises more easily.

You don't need this book if you fish the same three or four pools all season long, five days a week. You will know empirically where you can catch the most trout and the largest trout. *Reading Trout Streams* is for the fisherman who stands on the bank of an unfamiliar river or pool, confused, and asks: "Now what?"

Take everything you read in this book as suggestion, as prediction to where trout are most likely to be found. Trout can be *anywhere* in a river if conditions are right—and the next one you catch could make a fool out of me and everything I've written.

TOM ROSENBAUER
Manchester, Vermont
January 1988

1
A Trout's World

Trout have simple minds. But on a day when you can't catch a single one, even though they're feeding all around you, their brains swell to gigantic proportions. Man has made trout smart, praising their intelligence for hundreds of years. A sophisticated brown trout in the River Itchen in the famous chalkstream country in the south of England, whose ancestors have been fished over by generations of English aristocracy, is probably no smarter than a wilderness brook trout in Maine that has never seen a human and will strike a bare hook.

No doubt the brown trout will be harder to catch; he's a shyer species and he's probably learned something of man in his lifetime. His ancestors have grown up in an environment where there is plenty of food, and it's the individual who could feed most efficiently on drifting food that would get the best territory, survive to spawning, and mate with a similarly strong individual.

The wilderness brook trout's inclination to grab anything that drifts by him is no indication of his intelligence; it's a reflection of his environment. The cold, harsh, acidic world of a wilderness stream offers little food, and it's the fish that can eat anything that survives to spawning. The arrogant indices of intelligence that we apply to fish have little value, and if we look a little further than the stereotypes found in outdoor magazines we see that it's their needs, not their intelligence, that determine where and how they play our game.

An English chalk stream, with lush vegetation and sophisticated trout.

A wilderness brook trout stream is a harsh environment.

Simple minds have simple needs. All trout need food, shelter, and oxygen—assuming they have water. Those are the immediate needs. If a population is to be naturally reproducing or wild, they'll also need proper spawning habitat, which may or may need be the same as their ordinary living habitat. And they need deep pools or springs to spend the winter months, protected from anchor ice.

Few relationships in nature are anything close to linear. In order for trout to have food, there must be adequate oxygen, water temperatures, and nutrients to support the insects, crustaceans, and minnows they feed upon. Oxygen will depend on the water temperature and the amount of water surface that exchanges gas with the atmosphere—how much riffled water there is. Shelter means protection not only from predators but also a place to lie in the current, protected from it but with a food-carrying current within striking distance.

Taking a look at shelter first, you'll also discover that a trout's idea of a great place to live changes as he matures. The first place he lives is in a school of other tiny fry, barely an inch long, in shallow water. Here he's protected from the forages of larger fish, including his own parents, who would make a meal of him without a hint of guilt. As he matures and becomes a predator himself, at four or five inches, he'll establish a territory in deeper water, a place where he has the security of a nearby rock or log to swim to, but usually in the main current where he can grab drifting food. He may stay in this territory for the rest of his life, or he may switch to a better area as he gets older, larger, and more aggressive, displacing a less aggressive fish from an optimum spot. If he gets very large and develops a taste for other fish and crayfish, foregoing invertebrate diet, he may become what a biologist friend of mine calls a shark. Only a small percentage of a stream population becomes sharks, but those that do spend the daylight hours hiding under logs or undercut banks. Using their lateral line "hearing" as well as sight, they make feeding sprees at dusk, dawn, and even throughout the night, spearing into those shallows where the young-of-the-year fish have the advantage during the daylight hours, but not after dark or when the water clouds after a heavy rainstorm.

It's the middle fish, the drift feeder, that we're most interested in when we talk about reading a stream. He's the fellow that sits there waiting for your dry or nymph or wet to drift along to him. The shark, although he'll occasionally feed on insects during a heavy hatch, will usually be caught on a large wet fly or streamer after dark or during a rainstorm. He'll seldom feed from his territory but will cruise an entire pool when he's on the prowl; to catch him, you won't so much need to be able to read a stream as to be able to cover a lot of water—and overcome a fear of bats.

Shelter. Or territory. What does this mean? The territory a trout inhabits will be chosen by a delicate balance between the energy he expends for his meals, how much energy he obtains for his efforts, and how far he has to run when he's frightened or threatened. When bumbling around in a stream, we often see trout backed in under logs or rocks. They are there because we've frightened them into running there. They don't live in bolt holes. A trout can't get much food when he's crammed under a

Drift-feeding trout are the ones we're interested in when we talk about reading a stream.

log, no more than Londoners who spent nights in subway stations during the Blitz could get food.

You always hear about the ten-foot-deep pool in a river that "holds a trout as long as your leg." The big trout might be there, and it might be that the deep water has kept him safe for many years—but I'll bet you he doesn't do much of his feeding down there in the dark. There isn't much food on the bottom of a ten-foot pool. Depth only becomes important in a stream where there is no other place for a trout to hide when danger threatens. About three feet of water seems to be enough to give a trout complete security, since most of his enemies attack from above. You can test this hypothesis yourself by seeing how spooky a trout in a foot of water is compared to one that is in three feet of water. You can get a lot closer to the one in the deeper water.

So in a river where most of the pools and riffles are over three feet deep, depth will probably play a small part in where the trout live, and, conversely, in a stream that is barely ankle-deep in most places, even slight depth will be one of the most important factors. Still not convinced of the relative unimportance of depth in most trout streams? Look at the way a trout is built compared to the body shape of a sculpin: a trout is streamlined and his mouth faces forward and he's compressed laterally—a fish designed to feed in the middle to the top of the water column if ever there was one. Sculpins, on the other hand, are compressed dorsally for hanging near the bottom, and their mouths point down, so they can vacuum their food from the bottom.

A river's current is the conveyer belt that brings a trout his food. He sits in the open, or maybe under a branch or beside a log, but with easy access to the current. We like to call this his feeding lane but that term is misleading because the trout, if he can, will spend all his time here. It's his home. He'll defend this territory from other trout, but when he bolts to his logjam or rock pile, he'll allow all his neighbors who have been similarly frightened to crowd right in, fins touching.

Bob Bachman, an expert in brown trout behavior who did his PhD dissertation on wild brown trout feeding, has spent thousands of hours observing wild brown trout. He calls their feeding stations "seats in a restaurant" and it's an apt description. You can observe them, too, using polarized sunglasses to cut glare from the water's surface or by sneaking above them on a high bank or from a bridge. Another place to study their feeding behavior is, believe it or not, a trout hatchery—not in the concrete tanks but below the outflow of a hatchery. Most hatcheries use spring water, and in the outflow you'll always find a few escapees, feeding on excess food pellets in the water supply. They'll seldom spook at your approach because they're used to humans, so you can stand right beside them. Each fish will have his seat, usually in the main current, in front of or behind an obstruction, or where the bottom of the stream shows a slight depression. In these spots they're sheltered from the main current, so they don't have to work hard just to maintain their position, yet they have instant access to the current if a choice piece of food drifts by.

Watch what they do: they spot a food morsel, the fins wiggle a little, and as the food drifts overhead they tip their pectoral fins and drift upward to it. They don't swim. Just like a 727 taking off, they slide upward without a wriggle, pick up the tidbit, and tip down. The water pushes them back down to the bottom. In the process, the water pushes them back a couple of feet, and only after they're near the bottom again will they actually swim back upstream into position. It's a lazy and efficient way to feed, without a wasted motion.

When you watch a trout feeding, you'll also notice that there is little lateral motion. Choice pieces of food that are more than a foot from either side of his feeding lane are often ignored, especially if food is plentiful. Again, economy of motion. It's just too much work to jump off to the side and then fight the current to get back into position. But trout break the rules. Just when you thought you had his behavior figured out, he'll dart off to the side, two feet away, grab something with a splash and swim back to his position. Why? Maybe it was a bigger morsel, something too tempting to resist. You'll often see this move when food isn't plentiful, when a trout has to grab food that is farther away or go hungry. Young, inexperienced fish will often feed this way, dashing around, grabbing everything. But as food gets more abundant, even the little guys will settle down into a sedate, lazy, feeding rhythm.

The shape of a sculpin betrays its feeding habits.

So as you begin to read a stream, to pick up patterns, look for places where the main current, the smorgasbörd, flows. Then look for places that are slightly sheltered from the current. Look for spots where a trout can rest without even wiggling a fin, where, at the same time, he can watch for food drifting by and predators looming above him.

A trout at the moment of the rise—you don't see any splash because the motion is done with great economy.

Later I'll explore just where these feeding places are in a stream, but it's important to understand now that because of a trout's mind there is no way he's going to feed when he's crowded under a snag. His pea-brain doesn't allow him to do anything but be frightened and on his guard, and even if he could think about feeding he probably wouldn't. Feeding exposes him to dangers and betrays his position.

Oxygen, the other essential requirement for trout, is directly related to temperature. A trout needs at least three parts per million (ppm) of oxygen dissolved in water to survive. Colder water can hold more oxygen, so the lower temperature/higher oxygen limits are seldom limiting. It's when water gets above 75° that trout can suffocate, especially if there is little turbulence in the water to facilitate gas exchange with the atmosphere.

On a continuum, it looks something like this: at 32° to about 45°, a trout's metabolism is almost in a state of suspended animation, so his respiration requirements are minimal. And oxygen isn't a problem, anyway, because at these temperatures the water is often supersaturated with oxygen, up to 30 ppm. When the temperature rises above 50° their metabolism picks up and feeding activity increases greatly. At 55° to 65°, they're running in high gear—and their food, aquatic insects and crustaceans and minnows, is abundant. Oxygen is still no problem because even in a dead-slow pool, passive gas exchange provides plenty for respiration. This is the situation we most often encounter in the glory days of May and June in the East and Midwest, and June and July in the West. The fish are everywhere, they're feeding heavily, and we catch plenty if our presentation is correct.

Trouble starts somewhere between 68° and 75°, depending on the species of trout, how active it is, and how turbulent the water is—that is, how much white water and bubbles there are. The frothier the water, the more oxygen is getting into it. As the temperature climbs, two things happen: the amount of oxygen the water can hold decreases but the trout's metabolism increases at a furious rate. He's burning up that precious oxygen that gets scarcer as the sun gets higher. If the temperature gets too high, he'll suffocate.

Trout react to this danger first by decreasing their activity levels. You'll most often see this in the dog days of summer when daytime water temperatures climb into the 70s. The fish will just sulk on the bottom, and nothing will induce them to feed, not even your favorite Black Ant or Letort Hopper. They may take a few spinners at dusk but water takes a long time to give off heat, so evening water temperatures will almost be

White water at the head of this pool will keep the dissolved oxygen content high.

at a maximum. After dark the "sharks" will be ambushing minnows and crayfish, and if there's a moon the drift feeders may do some surface feeding. Remember that 95 percent of the trout population are sight feeders.

Early morning on these hot muggy days is a much better bet, because water temperatures then are at a minimum.

Trout have ways of circumventing high water temperatures. They have a strong avoidance reaction to uncomfortable temperatures—so they move. Sometimes it's just a few yards from the tail to the head of a pool, where the tumbling water coming in has more oxygen. If there is a spring entering the river nearby, the trout will be ganged up downstream of its plume, because groundwater can be 10° or even 15° cooler than surface flows. Sometimes just a steep shaded bank, or a ledgerock with a tiny trickle, will provide enough relief to attract many trout. I'll deal with ways to identify these spots in a later chapter.

So which of a trout's needs is most important? All things being equal, which will decide where you'll find them in a stream? In a way, shelter is both the most and the least important. In the Firehole River, probably the world's weirdest and most interesting trout stream because it's fed by many kinds of thermal springs, I've seen scores of brown trout grouped around the outflow of a cold spring. Right across the river were bubbling hot springs, and it was August, so the trout ran to the only place where

The Firehole, a trout stream that is fed by both cold and hot springs.

the water was cold enough to have sufficient oxygen to support them. I've also seen large, spooky wild brown trout leave secure places in brush piles along a bank to feed over a sandy flat barely ankle-deep. At midday. In August. During the fall spawning season, brook trout will move up through a riffle with their backs out of the water under bright sunlight—although browns and rainbows seem to be more circumspect and move at night.

All of these fish, although they appear to be oblivious of danger, will bolt for cover if severely frightened. If they're interested in feeding or desperate for cool water, they may be difficult to frighten, and they may come back soon—but that bolt hole is of utmost importance, whether it's a log or a rock or just an area of deeper water.

If you were a biologist you'd say that shelter was most important to a trout with temperature/oxygen second—for a trout can go for days or even weeks without food and still survive. But it's food, or the ease of obtaining it, that is really most important to us fly fishermen. If a trout is too frightened or too stressed for oxygen, he's not going to eat, and if he doesn't open those jaws we're not going to catch him.

So it doesn't matter to us that the big old brown trout just below the culvert on Mill Brook rests on the bottom in ten feet of water during the day if he doesn't feed there. It's academic. If he feeds at the tail of the culvert pool at dawn and dusk—that's a nugget. Then we try to figure out *why* he feeds there, so we can apply what we've learned to find other big brown trout. Look at the surface currents: slowest at the tail of the pool, and because the tail is narrower the food gets concentrated in a narrower path. Just above our trout there is also a small projection coming off the right bank, which bounces food toward him like a billiard ball coming off a cushion. There is also a log along the right bank, half submerged, that he can run to when you make a stupid move.

Then look a little closer. See *through* the water. There is a little whirl on the surface just below our friend's position. That whirl suggests something larger than the average bottom particle. Imagine yourself sinking below the surface, in that noisy world filled with silver pearls of air. Now you see his rock. It's shaped roughly like an equilateral triangle with each side about two feet long. There's a slight projection on the upstream point of the rock, smoothed by years of subaqueous sandblasting. That's where he rests his head. That's where he's protected from the current.

And now you're reading a trout stream.

2
Currents and Rocks

CURRENTS

Currents move around every living thing. As you sit reading this, air currents move around you—from open windows, from your own movements, from heat rising from a register. Air currents seldom affect us unless they're from a hurricane, because air is not very dense in relation to our body weight.

Streams have currents that affect a trout's every movement. A trout won't stroll around a pool without good reason, because this takes too much energy. Unless he's running from a predator, chasing a minnow, or migrating to a spawning area, current makes him a homebody. Think what your life would be like if you were constantly living in a 60 mph windstorm. You'd be a lot more careful about where you sat down to dinner.

Water moves downhill because of gravity; the steeper the slope, the faster it moves. Pools are areas where water velocity is decreased, either because the slope is gentler or because there is an obstruction blocking the flow of water. Runs and riffles are areas where water is flowing faster. Mountain rivers move faster than meadow brooks because their slope is steeper; lowland rivers that run through flat land move slowly.

Moving water is affected by friction. We can break down the flow of water into two modes: laminar and turbulent. In laminar flow, all the molecules of water move parallel to each other in a single direction. In turbulent flow, there are countless little eddies and whirlpools that move the water in all directions as the main current moves downstream.

The flow in the tail of this slow pool is nearly laminar.

Turbulent flow in a mountain river.

Water moving slowly through a polished steel tube is almost completely laminar. But as you increase the velocity of the water, friction between the water molecules and the sides of the tube produces tiny amounts of turbulence, and the faster the water flows, the greater the turbulence. If you imagine a trout stream with nearly smooth banks and bottom, the current moves at the same speed except for a small area near the banks and bottom. This is called the boundary layer, an area of turbulence where the downstream velocity is nearly zero. Add some tiny stones to the bottom of the channel and this boundary layer becomes larger, in proportion to the size of the stones—and also to the velocity of the main current. The faster the current, the greater the turbulence and the larger the boundary layer.

If the water is moving fast enough and/or the sizes of the objects on the bottom are large enough, the turbulence will be betrayed by disturbances carried to the surface of the water. This is what most people think of when they imagine being able to read a stream. Reading trout water is this—and much more.

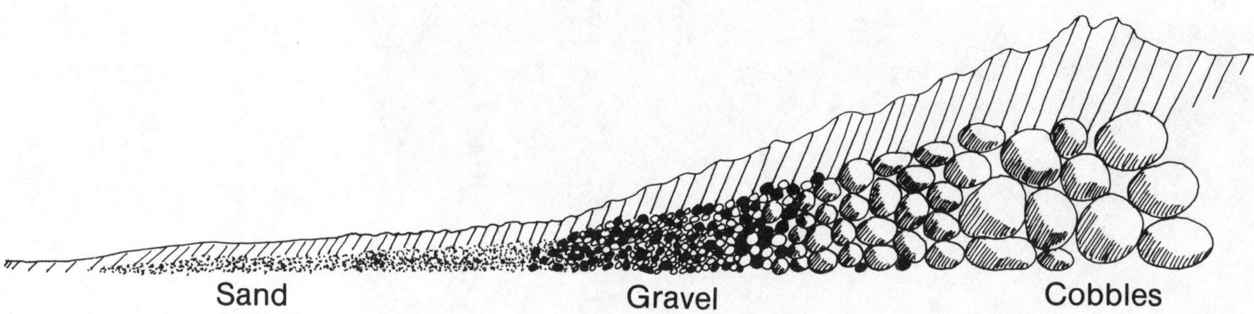

As the particle size on the bottom increases, the boundary layer (the lined area) gets bigger. The rougher the bottom, the more trout a stream can hold.

Forces besides friction also affect currents. The law of fluid dynamics, a principle of physics that neither you nor I want to bother thinking about when we're fishing, affects the currents. This principle has to do with the conservation of momentum, and two facts are of interest to us when we're looking for trout: water does not like to bend around corners, and when the velocity of water decreases its pressure increases. Let's take a look at a boulder lying in midstream and see what happens.

Bumps, Cushions, Dead Spots, and Focal Points

When water hits the front of the boulder, it stops. It bounces in all directions—back into the current, toward the bottom, and toward the surface. Pressure increases because of the great decrease in velocity, and if the water is shallow enough, the increase in pressure pushes the surface of the water up. A visible bump forms on the surface, and a very fast current may even produce a standing wave. The boundary layer in front of the rock is greatly increased because the water molecules pile up. Imagine yourself shoveling a thin layer of wet snow across your driveway. If you push a pile of it into a rock, some of it piles up in front of the rock and doesn't go any farther. I like to call this area of almost zero downstream velocity "the cushion."

Now let's look at the downstream side of the rock. Because moving water doesn't bend around corners, there is a dead spot behind the rock, again in proportion to the size of the obstacle. This dead spot would go on forever downstream, but because the faster water that has moved around the sides of the rocks has a lower pressure than the dead water behind it, water will move from the dead spot into the main current. Turbulence forms. The two currents mix. Just as you can see the bump that signifies the front of the rock on the surface, you can see the turbulence formed behind it. The turbulence is usually in a roughly triangular shape—its width tapers off as the turbulence loses energy with the downstream flow.

The bump just ahead of it and the turbulence below it reveal the position of this midstream rock.

The same sort of thing happens when current flows over a depression in the stream bed, or where it spills over from a shallow riffle into a deeper pool. The current keeps on moving downstream parallel to the shallower upstream bottom, forming a dead spot below it—but the area of higher pressure in the dead spot moves toward the higher-velocity water with lower pressure, producing turbulence and eventually mixing the two parcels of water together.

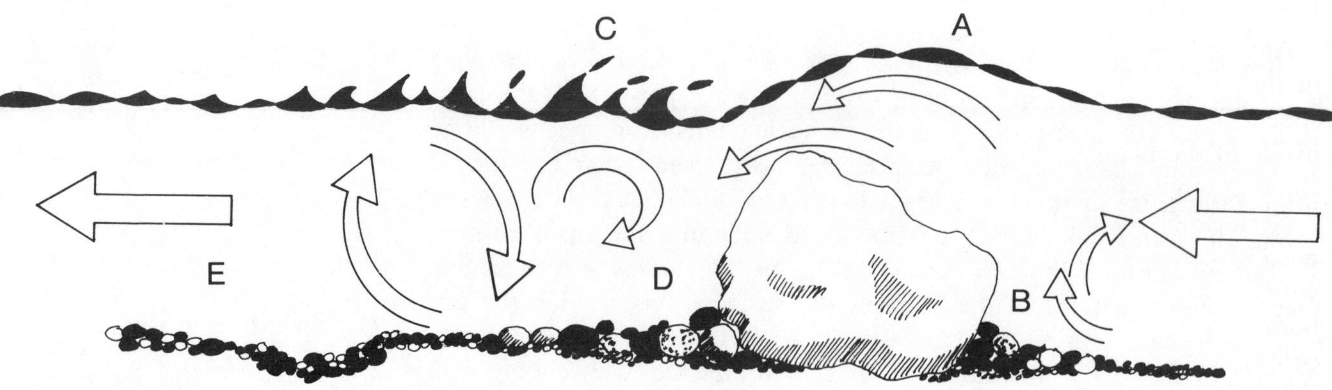

Currents around a submerged rock. The bump at A indicates the cushion, B. The turbulence behind the rock, C, is above the dead spot at D. E is the focal point, where the turbulence lessens.

A trout lying at the lip of a shelf is protected from the force of the current, but he can tip into the current for his food. The surface of the water is more turbulent where water flows over a shelf.

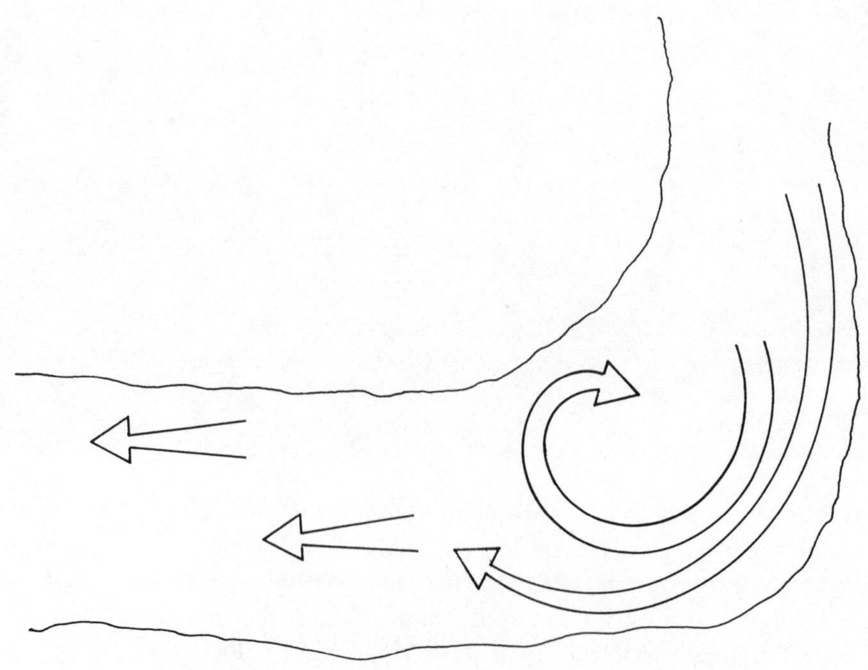

A whirlpool is often formed on the inside of a sharp bend.

Another physical force comes into the picture when currents hit a bend in the river: centrifugal force. Water whipping around a bend picks up speed on the outside or concave bend, and a "seam" is formed on the inside of the bend where the velocity is greatly decreased. If the angle is sharp enough, a whirlpool will be formed at the "elbow" of the bend.

Because of friction and the turbulence caused by it, current is slower, not only near the bottom, but near the banks as well. Water in contact with the banks causes a slowing down of current just as it does near the bottom, so a cross-section of a river will show the fastest current near the center of the surface, with the velocity decreasing as you move away from this point. This is assuming that a deep center channel is surrounded by banks that slope gently upward. In a bend in the river, where the fastest current swings toward one bank, there will be a steep gradient from a current maximum on the deeper or concave bank, with a more gradual slope and current deceleration toward the shallower, slower bank.

Because the lower-velocity water near the bank has a higher pressure than the faster moving water in the center, things that fall into the water get pulled into the current. The phenomenon has a significance to trout. Grasshoppers, ants, and beetles that fall into the water get pulled into the main current, so they're available to trout in all areas of a river, not just to those that live near the banks and under trees.

Where Trout Live

Studies have shown that trout prefer to lie in water that runs about one-quarter to one-half foot per second and feed in water that runs about two feet per second. So we're looking for places where there is a slow current bordered by a slightly faster current. Imagine a trout sitting in a little pocket in front of a rock or along a shelf, with just enough current to bathe his gills with oxygen, darting upward or sideways into the faster current to feed. He needs this faster current because water that's running at one-half foot per second may not deliver food at a fast enough rate.

To put these speeds into perspective, the center channel of a brawling western river like the Madison might be running at ten or twelve feet per second. A trout that had to dart into the current this fast would get knocked downstream each time he fed, and would soon waste away from a tremendous loss of energy. The maximum velocity that a trout will feed in seems to be about six feet per second, and rainbow trout are more inclined to feed in a very fast current than brooks, browns, or cutthroats. Even so, a fish that has to fight a five-foot-per-second current had better be getting some big, high-protein morsels like giant stoneflies or grasshoppers for his efforts.

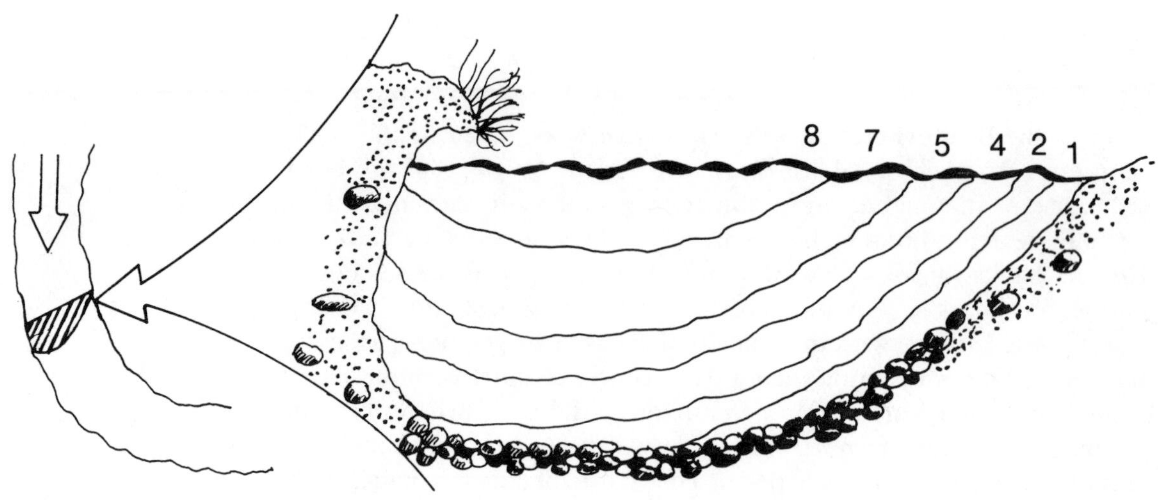

Cross-section of a river showing velocities in feet per second in a straight stretch and at a bend. Can you see why trout lie on the bottom and near the banks? Note the undercut bank at the outside of the bend—but also that the preferred one-foot-per-second velocity is not present at the outside of the bend.

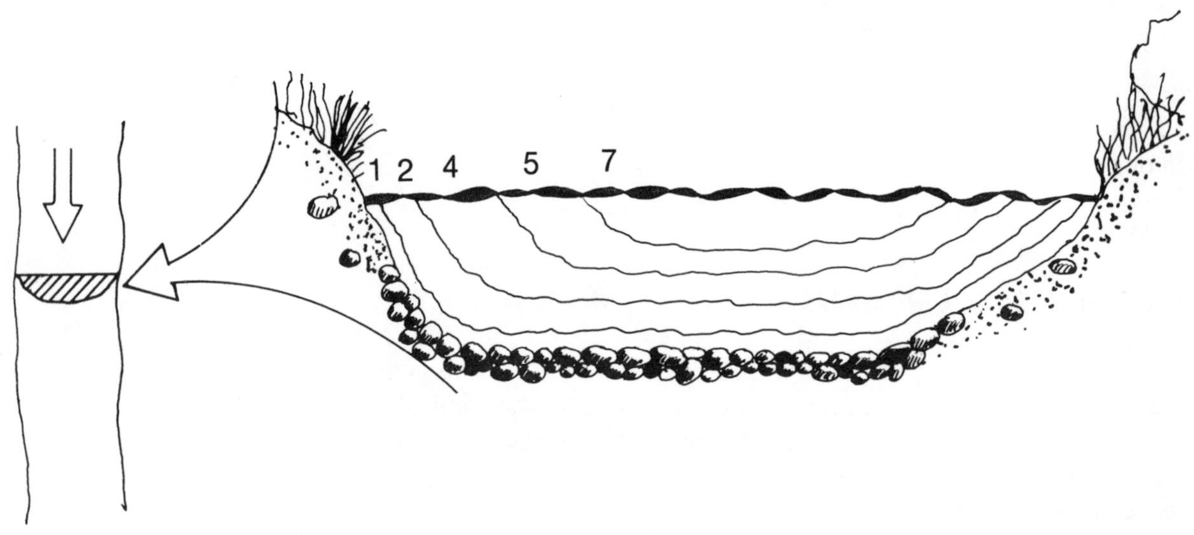

The next time you're near a river, take a ping-pong ball, a piece of duct tape, and a ten-foot length of string with you. Tape the string to the ball, drop it into the water, and time how long it takes to straighten the string. Divide by ten and you have a fair estimate of the current velocity. Do this in the fastest and the slowest places you can find to get an idea of the range of velocities in your stream. An alternative that you can try when you're fishing is to cast straight upstream with a floating line, gathering line as the current brings it to you, as if you were fishing a dry fly. Watch your stripping hand. See how much line you gather in one second. This will surely give you a ballpark figure on stream velocities—and it will make you look at a river as you never did before.

The Madison. The current in the middle of the river might be moving at ten feet per second; a trout's only relief from the current would be the three rocks, two submerged and one partially submerged—except, of course, for the area near the banks.

This chapter is about objects in the water and where you'll find trout in relation to them. In some streams you'll be able to read and fish to each discrete resting spot because you can see these spots: in small streams, in shallow rivers, and in pocket water where there are really no defined pools, just miniature pools formed by rocks and logs. This is like micro stream-reading, as opposed to macro stream-reading; here you see patterns of currents that are formed by large groups of rocks or bends in a river or a sudden change in the slope of the stream bed—things that form what we call pools.

Midstream Rocks

Let's take the simplest case, that of a rock in midstream. We'll make the river two feet deep and the rock, a round one, four feet in diameter—so half of the rock sticks above the surface. Just ahead of the rock you'll see the little bump caused by the piling of water in the cushion. You also spot another clue to how large it is—a patch of sand. Most of the bottom here is gravel and rock. Because sand is fine, it gets carried out of the faster water and is deposited in slow pools. Because the dead spot is slower water, sand falls out of the current here—in fact you can often spot it ahead of a submerged rock before you see the rock itself. Sand is lighter in color than most bottoms so it flashes a warning that there is slower current here, and perhaps a nice trout.

The light patch of sand on the downstream (right) side of this rock shows the area of reduced velocity.

Trout like to lurk in front of rocks for another reason. During times of fast current flow, the higher pressure and turbulence formed in front of the rock dig into the gravel of the river bed, making a little depression. A trout positioned in front of a rock not only has a slower current but also a good place from which to spot objects coming toward him; and he has a little spot to snuggle into while he waits for food.

Cracker barrel discussions, when trout fishermen get together, sometimes center around the question: "Do trout prefer to live ahead of or behind rocks?" Between my own observations and constant grilling of fishing buddies around the country, it's about a 50-50 proposition, and in most cases the trout like both choices. We can argue all we want—it's the trout's vote that counts.

In some streams trout are found in great numbers behind rocks, but in very specific places. In the rock we were just looking at, for instance, I wouldn't expect to find a trout immediately behind the rock, at least not in the center of the eddy. Because the rock is quite large, there is really no current flow just behind it, so there's no food being brought to the trout. This is an especially barren place for food because the top of the rock is above the water, so food that floats straight into the face of the rock gets shoved to either side. And that's an obvious clue as to where we'll find the trout.

As the current is funneled around either side of the rock, its speed increases around the smooth sides, so we wouldn't expect to find trout there. But as we get below the rock, there is a spot on either side where the dead spot borders the current sweeping around the rock. The line between the turbulent water behind the rock and the main current is very

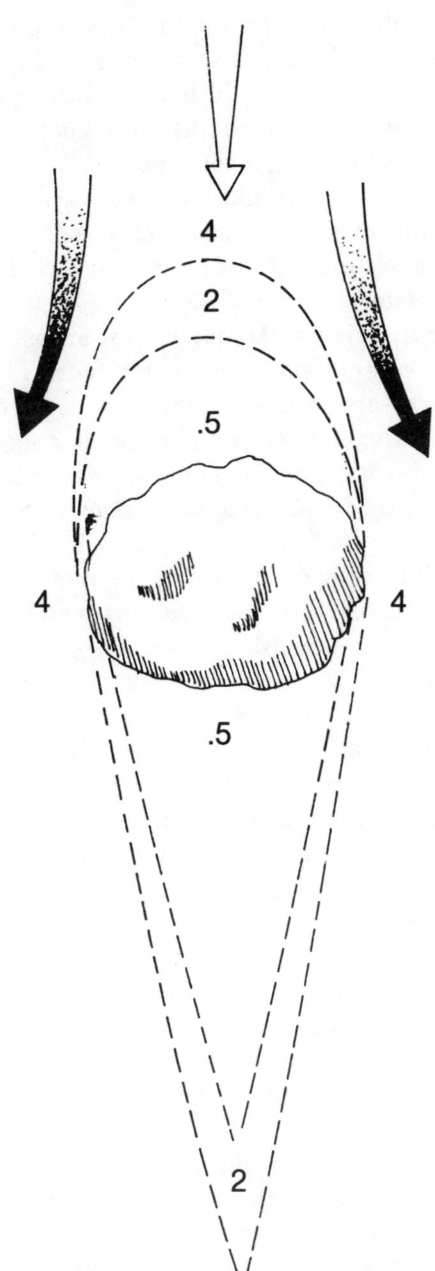

Approximate current speeds around a partially submerged rock in a four-foot-per-second current. Trout prefer to lie in currents that are about one-half foot per second and feed in currents that are about two feet per second.

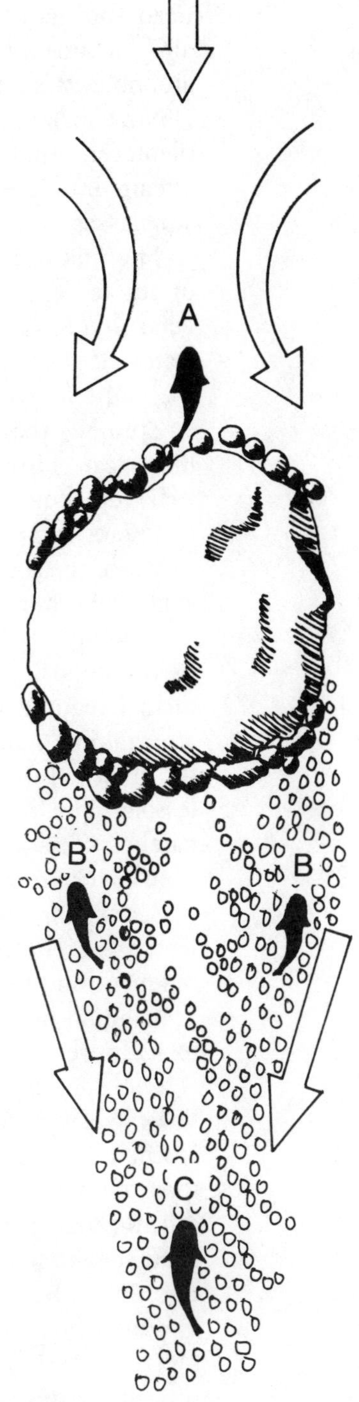

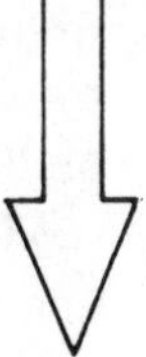

Possible lies around a partially submerged rock. The trout at A is lying in the cushion in front of the rock; the two trout at B are just outside of the dead spot; and the fish at C is in the focal point, probably the best spot.

apparent, and this edge is a comfortable place for a trout to position himself, where he can observe all that food floating just inches away. As the dead spot narrows to a point below the rock, you'll find the best spot of all—an area of reduced flow, yet with the food that has been swept around *both* sides of the rock coming to a single focal point.

Now make the river here three feet deep and the rock two feet in diameter. First you have to find the rock. Let's say you're looking upstream into the intense glare of a setting sun, so even with polarized sunglasses you can't see into the water.

The first thing you'll spot is the turbulence. It may be just a small area of surface current that whirls ever-so-subtly for just a few feet. This is what you'll see if the current isn't very fast, or if the rock is in deep water. If the current is moving briskly, say six or eight feet per second, the sudden change in pressure may even push a standing wave into the air, plumes that get caught in upstream winds, blowing spray that looks like a car going the wrong way on the L.A. Expressway.

If you look closely, you'll be able to spot the bump that marks the upstream end of the rock—approximately. The main current is still going to push the bump and the turbulence downstream, so things will be slightly farther upstream than you think.

As mentioned before, in many streams you can spot a submerged rock by the deposits of lighter-colored sand in front of and especially behind a rock. I learned to wade the Ausable in upstate New York the hard way, after taking many swims as a teenager. Finally, an old-timer yelled across the river, "Jump to the light spots, young man," and I never forgot his lesson. The rocks in this river are round, large, and slippery, but the patches of sand behind them are a secure foothold, as well as a haven from fast currents.

Everything that makes the head of a partially submerged rock a trout haven also holds true for one that is fully submerged. Find the turbulence, find the bump, then lead the bump with your cast by a few feet. You should be drifting your fly right over a trout. The tail of a submerged rock, however, is a different story.

The spot behind a fully submerged rock is different because water flows over the top of the rock as well as around the sides. Of course, there is still a dead spot just behind it, and in some respects this is a better spot than one below a rock that sticks above the surface. Not as much of the drifting food gets pushed aside, so the area just below the rock can be a good spot to live. In currents that are slow to moderate, the whole area of turbulence below a submerged rock is prime trout territory.

But in fast currents, with rocks bigger than bowling balls, life can be pretty rugged just behind the rock. When fast-moving water coming over the top of the rock meets dead water just below the rock, the resulting turbulence can be so violent that a standing wave forms. The last thing a trout wants is to be pushed constantly toward the surface. A fish that has to work to stay near the bottom will starve to death—or, if he's smart, he'll move elsewhere.

Most trout fishermen know that trout lie behind rocks but too many are unaware of the finer points. I know I was until a float trip on the Madison a few years ago. Floating below Wolf Creek with guide John Keiser, I

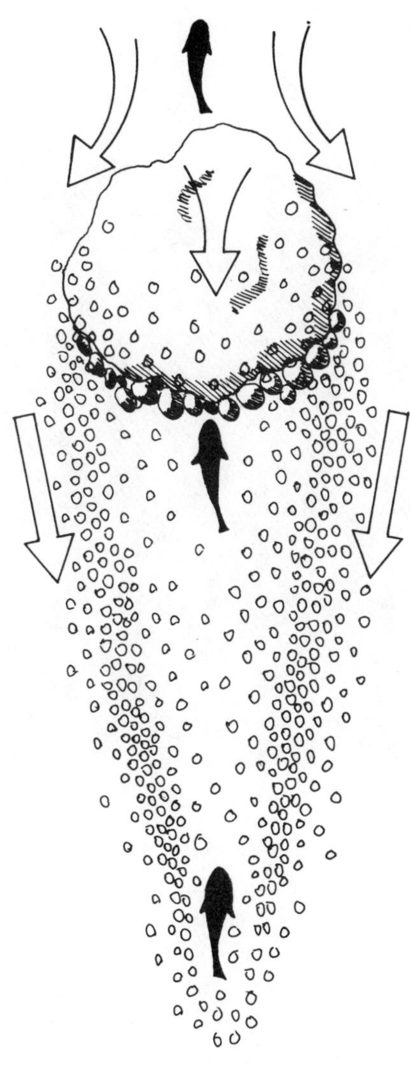

Possible lies around a fully submerged rock in moderate current. The fish behind the rock can stay right in the dead spot because food is being washed over the top of the rock.

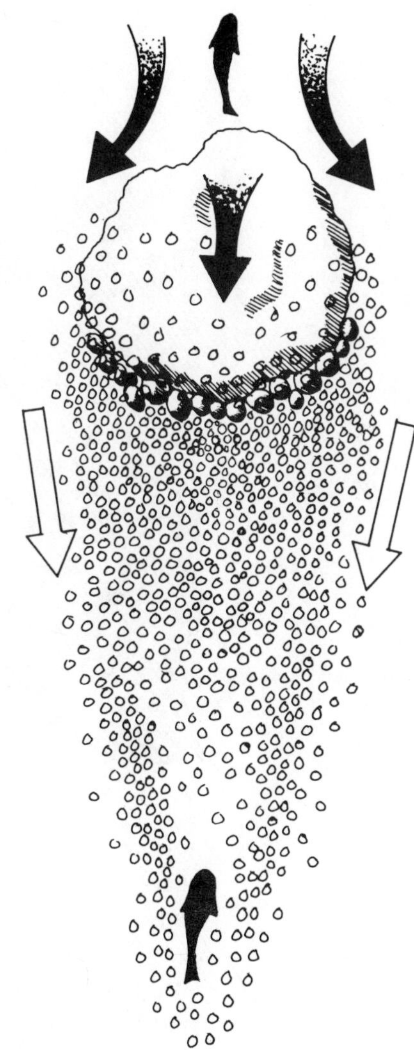

Lies around a fully submerged rock in fast current. There are no trout immediately behind the rock because the turbulence there is too intense.

kept trying to find the big rainbows that like the middle channel of this archetypal boulder-strewn river. When you're float fishing, you hit the exact spot you expect to find a fish, leading it by just enough to let the fish get a look at your fly. You only have one chance. I kept hitting the slicks right behind the rocks, and didn't have enough time to get in a cast in the plume ten feet downstream. "Try a little lower in the slick," John suggested, and as soon as I put the fly half-way down the turbulence I began hooking fish. When I asked him why, John allowed as how the rainbows probably get "knocked around" too much just below the rocks, and prefer the tamer water below.

The intense turbulence below this rock shows why trout may not always be found directly behind a rock.

John's remarks clicked with something Bob Bachman told me that year—"Trout like things predictable, they don't like surprises"—and the idea has changed the way I fish to rocks. Trout don't like places with *strong* eddies or swirls, because they can't stay still; even more importantly, they can't predict the trajectory of the food supply. (Imagine if your fork only found its way to your mouth 25 percent of the time.) When you look at turbulence anywhere in a stream, spend less time fishing the areas of harsh turbulence. Concentrate on the more comfortable areas in front of or behind it.

It's good practice to look at individual rocks in the water and how they affect currents and trout, though you seldom find one rock alone. The geology and slope that lead one rock to its position accumulate others of roughly the same size. If the bed of the river is nearly blanketed with boulders, you get what fishermen call "pocket water." At first glance, such water looks inhospitable to fish—churning and frothing everywhere. Most of the water's power, though, is dissipated in all directions over and around the rocks rather than just channeled downstream, and the current in most areas of pocket water is slower than placid-looking flats in other areas of the river.

Because there are so many good places to live, pocket water is one of the most productive kinds of trout water. There can actually be "a fish behind every rock." The late Ray Smith, a famous Catskill fly tier who specialized in the Esopus and Schoharie, used to call the fish in pocket water on the Schoharie "woodchuck fish." They'd poke their noses out from holes between the rocks for a dry fly, even in midsummer when the Schoharie is considered unfishable because of high water temperatures.

Pocket water looks inhospitable at first glance, but it offers many places for trout to live.

An abundant supply of oxygen in the turbulence kept the Schoharie woodchuck fish healthy, when the fish from the big pools had all migrated to spring holes.

When you choose your casts in water where there are a lot of rocks, look for places where the prime spot of one rock intersects with a likely spot in another. Does the place where the plume behind one rock comes together intersect the cushion upstream of another rock? Is there a basketball-sized rock wedged at the edge of a plume below a huge boulder? Either of these would be my choice for extra attention. In the same light, one rock can have a negative reinforcement of another. The basketball-sized rock, normally a good size for holding a trout, would probably be worthless if it were located behind a boulder that could hide a small elephant. The water directly behind an obstruction that size will be practically devoid of current and food.

Another way to fish pocket water is to look for the central current; unless the water is completely boulder-strewn you can find the unbroken, faster center channel that exhibits less turbulence. This part of the river may be too fast for the trout but the rocks that touch its margins will probably be the most productive areas. Those rocks are closer to the steady food supply provided by the center channel's conveyer belt.

In rivers like the Madison, the Housatonic, and the upper Connecticut on the Vermont/New Hampshire border, you find a lot of water with a strong central current and boulders right up against the banks. I've spent some fruitless hours struggling to wade among these tricky boulders, casting into the main current. Only a heavy Hendrickson hatch on the Housatonic showed me the error of my ways one late-April day. My wife,

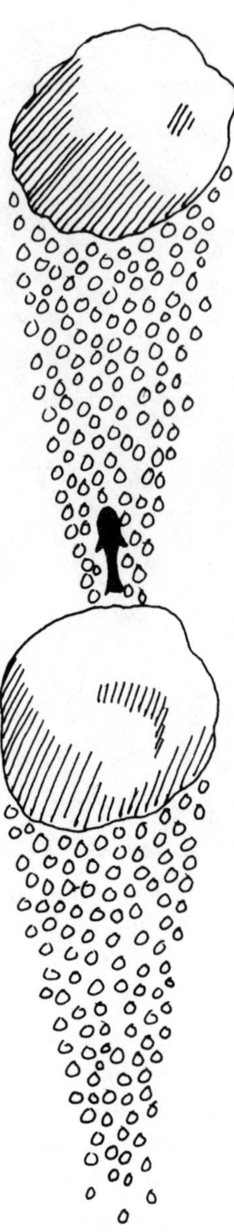

Where there are many rocks in the river bed, look for places where the focal point of one rock intersects the cushion of another.

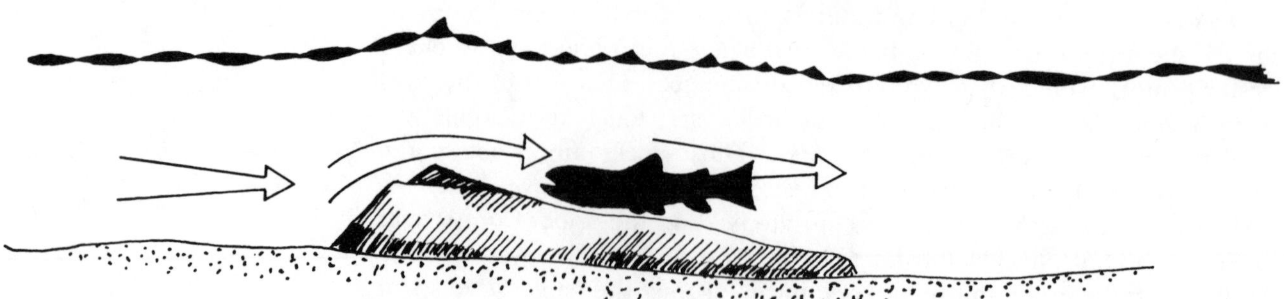

A trout using a flat rock for a pillow. This kind of lie is often found toward the tail of a pool.

who stayed out of the heavier water, cleaned up by barely getting her feet wet. Her macho husband waded between the boulders and spooked more fish than he hooked.

Thus far we've assumed that the rocks in a river bed are more or less round. What about flat rocks? Flat rocks will hold trout as long as they aren't recessed into the river bed like flagstones and thus don't break the current. In fact, trout like to live on top of flat rocks, especially those that are tipped slightly. The greater a flat rock is tipped either forward or backward in relation to the current, the larger the cushion it will form. I've seen many trout, especially those in the tails of flat pools, lie on top of flat rocks that have their leading edges tipped slightly forward. The trout use the leading edge of the rock as a pillow, letting their bodies slip into the cushion of slower water behind.

Ledgerock

In an area with a lot of flat rocks on the bottom, you'll find trout on top of, in crevices between, ahead of, and behind the rocks. Sometimes the bed or bank of the river is actually composed of bedrock, a condition fishermen call ledgerock. This kind of geology looks pretty but it can be very disappointing because of its paucity of aquatic life.

An old Vermonter once told me about a river on the New York State border that had cut a deep canyon through a valley. "Park at the cemetery and hike down over the hill," he said. "You'll find it real pretty." I spent an entire May afternoon, at the peak of a Hendrickson hatch, fishing the canyon. I caught no trout and hardly saw a fly. But I was fascinated by the huge flat sheets of slate that made up the bottom of the river. Some of the sheets stretch unbroken across the bottom for over a hundred feet. When I next saw the old fellow I told him I hadn't gotten a single trout in the canyon. "I didn't tell you there were many trout in there," he said. "All I told you was that it was pretty. Where the hell are the trout going to sit, and where are the bugs going to live? First flood'd wash 'em away."

I've been back to that canyon a few times, and I have found some trout. Wherever there is a break in the bedrock and a little pool with some gravel deposited in it, there is a concentration of trout. I might have to walk through a half-mile of barren water to find these little treasures between the bedrock—but the isolation and the scenery of canyon water always make it worthwhile.

Bedrock can also intersect a stream vertically, forming sheer banks, ledges, and deep pools below. Most trout streams, especially those in the East, have at least one ledgerock pool and in some small brooks these are the only places where the stream collects any depth. Despite their beauty, I've sometimes been disappointed by ledgerock banks.

Take your eyes off that cool, rhododendron-lined bank and look below the surface. Current usually strikes ledgerock banks at an obtuse angle, sometimes even close to a 90-degree change in direction of flow.

This bedrock pool on Kettle Creek in Pennsylvania does not offer much to either trout or insect life.

If the bank was made of a material that eroded easier, like gravel or sand, a meander might develop. But ledgerock banks are solid and can deflect the current even at a full right angle without yielding more than a few pebbles each year. So the water swats up against the unyielding rock, then follows the ledge downstream at relatively full force, until the ledge ends. There is little turbulence on the ledge side, because the smooth bank just lets the water slip along. You'll find a cushion right up against the ledge, but it is seldom wide enough to afford a living space for a trout.

If the ledge isn't completely smooth, there may be places tight against it that will hold trout. A little cove cut into the sharp edge, or perhaps a stubborn edge that hasn't been worn away by hundreds of years of nonstop current, will form a dead spot, as long as the depression or projection extends near or to the bottom. There might even be a second tier of ledge that extends out from the bank underwater—a close look at the surface currents along the wall should tell you. An area of turbulence along a smooth rock face tells you there is something under the water that is blocking the current and perhaps holding a fat brookie.

I know that sheer rock wall still looks good, with a deep dark hole beneath it, but where are the trout in that hole going to get their food? There might be a large brown trout that hides in the depths all day long coming out at night to feed, but notice I said *coming out to feed.* He's not eating down there, he's hiding or sleeping. There are no minnows in the deep and few insects. Take a look at a couple of other spots that, although they might look less tantalizing, may hold some feeding trout.

Opposite to the point where the current first hits the ledge will be what is called a seam, a spot that receives much of the debris carried by the current but little of its force. There is a seam on the inside of every bend in the river, and it's clearly a prime spot, with lots of food, yet easy living. At this point, there is ordinarily a drop-off in depth, so a trout can also have the benefit of a further reduction in flow without sacrificing his meal ticket. I've risen many more fish in the seam than I have against the bank on the opposite side.

Now as you follow the current downstream, you'll see its force start to slow about halfway down the ledgerock. Friction is finally coming into play, as is a little bit of centrifugal force, introduced when the stream turned the bend against the ledgerock, now pulling some of the current back toward the center of the stream. Here, where the full force of the current starts to break, there will be more trout. Anywhere there is a projection off the bottom or a section of ledgerock poking into the current can be a hot spot. But the best is yet to come.

Where the ledgerock bank ends is always the beginning of something that is eroded more easily—a different type of bedrock, sand, gravel, or mud. Water sweeps off the end of the bedrock, finds a dead spot where the current has eaten into the bank, and there you have a spot of turbulence. You also have the best spot along a ledgerock bank.

The trailing edge of a ledgerock bank, on the right of this photo, is a prime spot for a trout.

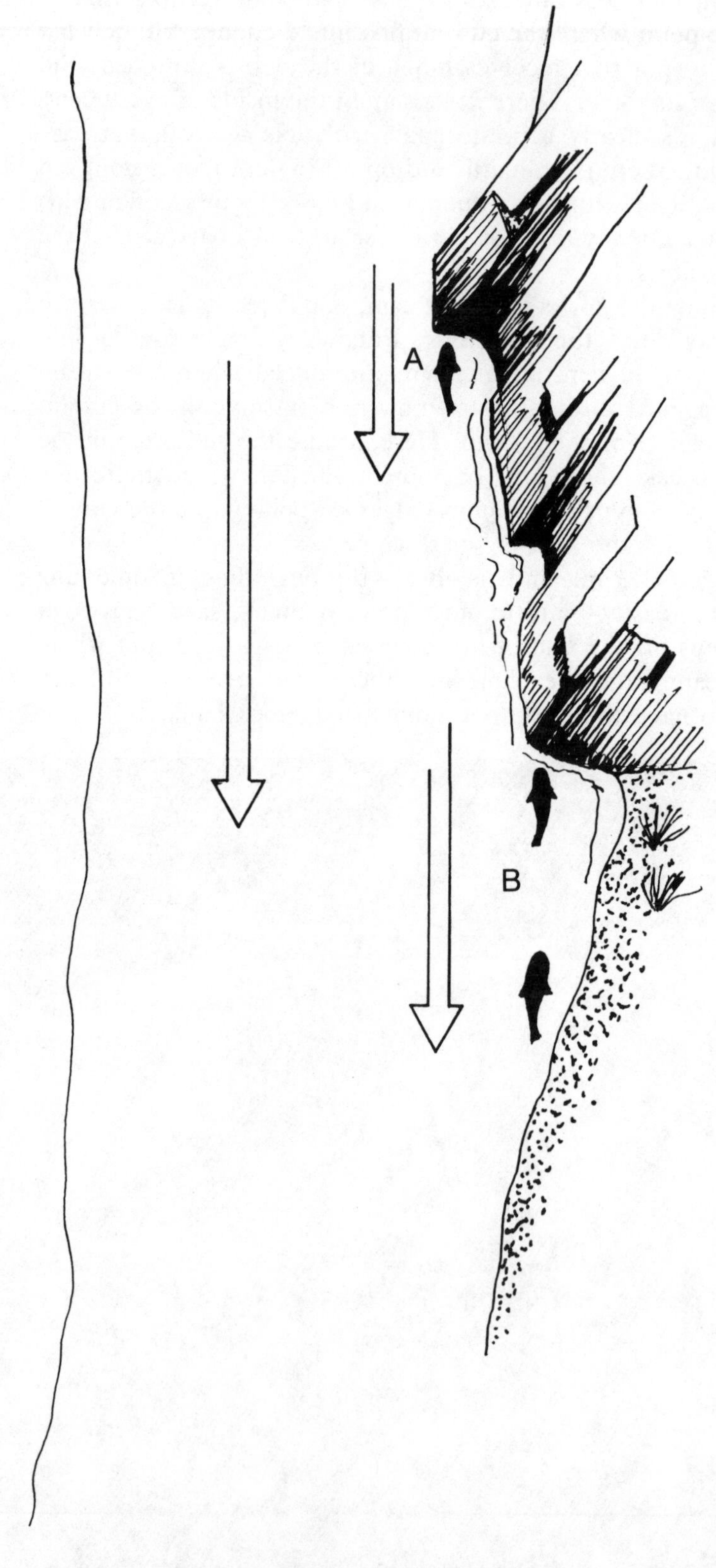

Possible lies along a ledgerock bank. The trout at A is just behind a point jutting out from the ledgerock. The two fish at B are in the best place, the seam below the end of the ledgerock.

In ledgerock sections on the upper Willowemoc in the Catskills or one of my little brooks in Vermont or the Fall River in Idaho, the best fish I've taken or spooked or seen rising have been just at the trailing edge of a ledgerock bank. You'll see a distinct line in the water where the current borders the dead spot downstream of the ledgerock. The trout will be just to the inside of that line, and sometimes there will be half a dozen queued up, all just inside the dead spot, for twenty or thirty feet downstream.

I'm not sure exactly why trout are so fond of the trailing edge of ledgerock when other spots in the same pool look more favorable. Perhaps the current flattened along the sheer wall carries a lot of food compressed into one little lane. And the ledgerock itself is a haven to which a trout can bolt when danger threatens, either into the clefts in its sides or the deep pool beneath.

Notice that I've hardly talked about pools and runs and riffles? They're just larger manifestations of the features I've already covered, produced by changes in slope or groups of rocks rather than single boulders. Many streams don't have large rocks, or certain stretches of them don't, so you have to read a stream by looking at larger parcels of water at one time. Don't worry, we'll talk about pools, bends, shelves, riffles, and runs after a chapter on an important part of stream reading that is often overlooked—the banks and objects above the water.

3
Other Features in and Around the Water

Rocks are the most important feature in most streams but other objects may attract or repel trout. In spring creeks, weeds are the dominant object in the water, but a trout's position near them is not as predictable as with rocks. Logs fall in the water and provide havens for trout. Looking at the banks of a trout stream may tell you more about where to find the trout than looking at the water. And manmade objects, whether they're placed in the water for trout, like deflectors and log dams, or whether they're for some "higher" purpose like highway bridges, can influence where you'll find trout.

Logs

Logs are more temporary structures than rocks in trout streams, especially if they fall into the water at an angle perpendicular to the current. This past spring, a violent windstorm uprooted a young maple and toppled it into the brook near my house. The tree originally landed right across the river, and I noticed that every time the water went up after a rainstorm, the log was pushed closer to the bank and more parallel to the current. I also realized that I didn't start seeing and catching trout near the log until it was parallel to the current.

Logs that stretch across the current, forming big swirls and eddies behind them, always look inviting. They seldom produce as many or as large a trout as you'd expect, especially downstream of the log. Why? There are a number of logical reasons, based upon what we've learned so far. One is that a log that stretches across the current is seldom a permanent structure.

Trout settle into one spot and may live there the entire season, sometimes for several seasons. A temporary structure may hold a trout that has been pushed there from another spot, but because the log hasn't been around for long, the chances are less of finding a decent trout living there. In small streams, logs lying across the current are more valuable, sometimes because a log in the current may form the only deep water and protection for twenty or thirty feet. A small stream will seldom produce enough current to move a log, and the log can be anchored in both banks. A log perpendicular to the current may be a permanent fixture in a small stream, and will be around long enough to accumulate a trout or two.

One very important kind of streamside log is called a sweeper. This is a tree that has fallen into the water, is attached to the bank and is sometimes still alive, and has a trunk that is halfway submerged. No trout stream in North America displays the form and value of the sweeper more than Michigan's AuSable. This river is rich in insect life, and has a very slow, stable current. It is lined with sweepers that may stay in place for years because the AuSable does not experience the severe floods that would wash the sweepers away in a typical freestone river. Rusty Gates, owner of Gates AuSable Lodge, is a superb fisherman who could fish miles of these sweeper-infested banks blind-folded. He once told me where he finds trout in relation to these sweepers.

"The fish will be lined up on the inside of the bubble line trailing downstream of the end of the sweeper," he said. "You'll seldom find many fish behind the log itself, I guess because there isn't much food there." We were looking at a quick sketch he had drawn of a sweeper. He stubbed his finger on the upstream side of the log, at the place where it is anchored to the bank, and said with great conviction, "And there is where you'll find a hog."

Why is fishing behind a log that stretches into the current not always productive? Watch what happens when a piece of floating debris drifts toward a log. It tarries a bit in front, then gets pushed around the end and away from the spot behind the log. And look at the current behind the log—the water forced over the top, if there is any running over the top, and the water forced underneath form a swirling, boiling, unpredictable eddy behind the log. This is a tough place for a trout to live and feed.

Around a perpendicular log, then, if there are trout they will probably be in front of the log or at both ends of the log, where food will accumulate and there is still some respite from the current. If there is a little "plunge pool" below the log, formed by the digging action of the current behind the log, you may also find trout closer to the tail of the plunge pool than to the log, because the current will flatten out and become more gentle and predictable as you go downstream from the log.

A log that lies parallel to the current is a much better place to look for trout. It has probably been there longer, because floods slip right past. It

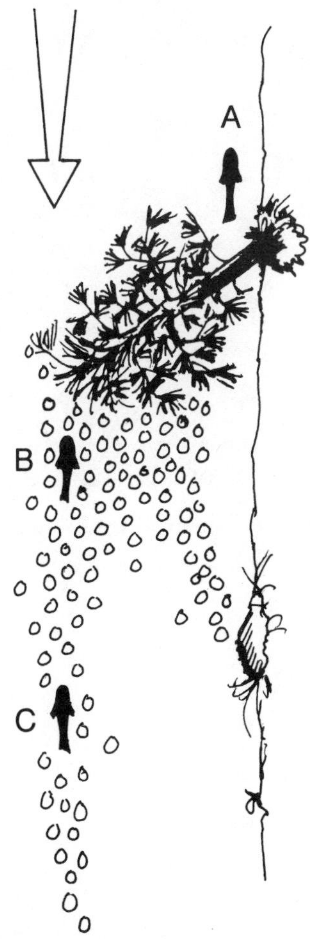

The best lies around a sweeper. The fish at A is often the largest. The trout at B and C are in the seam below the outside edge of the sweeper, and C is probably the smallest trout of the three.

Fishing to the upstream side of a sweeper.

Sweepers on Michigan's Au Sable. *Photo by Dennis Potter.*

This log lying parallel to the bank *must* hold a big trout.

may have been there for so long that it has become waterlogged, almost as permanent as the rocks on the bottom. One log on the Battenkill that regularly produces trout for me has been in the same spot along the bank for ten years, and it shows no sign of giving up its position.

Parallel logs don't create whirling turbulence, being in harmony with the current, but they do provide cushions of dead water—without pushing any food away. A waterlogged stump in the middle of a pool will betray its presence with turbulence if it is close to the surface and if the current is fast enough. Its disturbance will be long and slender, though, and if the water isn't clear enough for you to see the log you may mistake it for a small rock.

The cushion in front of a submerged log is usually not large enough to hold a trout, but both sides of the log have a cushion just wide enough to hold a decent fish. If a log were perfectly smooth, the cushion would be very small. However, logs are covered with bark and knobs and they're seldom perfectly straight, so a nice cushion forms along its length, especially on the inside of a curve or just below a little knob that projects out into the current. It's a perfect place because the trout's feeding spots and its refuge are the same, and when danger threatens, all it does is snuggle a little closer to the log.

Trout react to the color of a stream bottom and vary the shades of their body to blend in. If you move a pale trout from white sand to black basalt, it will darken its body in a matter of days. I've often caught trout alongside logs that were pale yellow on the side facing the current, and dark brown on the side that was constantly shaded by the log.

The dead spot just behind a log can also be good. Here food rushes by on either side, letting a trout choose its meal from either the left or the right. But because of the added attraction of shelter along the sides of the log, you'll probably find more and better fish along the sides than behind a parallel log.

I go out of my way to fish parallel logs that rest against the bank. My first trout over twenty inches came to a sulphur spinner just off the trailing edge of such a log, and I know there were two other trout rising beside the log that were larger, yet the log was only about seven inches in diameter and ten feet long. This attraction to logs along a bank is so strong that large trout may hold and feed in water that appears to be much too shallow. A couple of summers ago I was surprised when a brown trout close to twenty inches long pounced on a Letort Hopper that I slapped off the side of a log in a side channel of the Madison. There was no more than eight inches of water on the current side of the log—and not another decent piece of cover for thirty feet in either direction.

Favorite lies in a great spot—a log lying parallel to the bank. The trout will be found along the outside edge of the log and in the dead spot behind it.

Banks

In some rivers, more large trout are caught on flies within a foot of the bank than the remaining parts of the river combined. Banks provide shelter, food, and protection from the current—but some part of the main current, the buffet line, must flow nearby. A quick glance at a section of river can usually tell you if the banks are any good.

Look at the slope of the land around a river. If the land is flat and banks are made from wide gravel bars without any vegetation, you can assume that if there are any trout near that bank, they cruise in occasionally to feed in the evening but probably don't live there. If, on the other hand, the land on the other side of the river drops steeply into the river and there are trees and shrubs and big rocks along the bank, there may be some nice places for trout.

Those are the two extremes. When should you wade the middle of a river and fish into the banks, or creep along the bank casting straight upstream or downstream? When should you wade near the banks and cast to the center of the river?

First, look for the bubble or drift line. This indicates the main current—that water which is passing most rapidly through a pool. It's also the part of the river carrying the most food. This part of the stream may split, however, and there may be two "main currents" or three or half a dozen. If any part of the bubble line touches either bank, and there is more than six inches of water along the bank, you have a spot that is at least worth looking into a little further.

Next take a glance at the rest of the river. Are there some big rocks in the center, or groups of smaller rocks? The Battenkill and the Henry's Fork at the Railroad Ranch are hardly similar rivers. The Henry's Fork is rich in food, wide, and full of weeds. Battenkill trout grow slowly, the river is small, and the bottom is covered with fine gravel. Both rivers, however, give the impression of smoothness, because there are few large

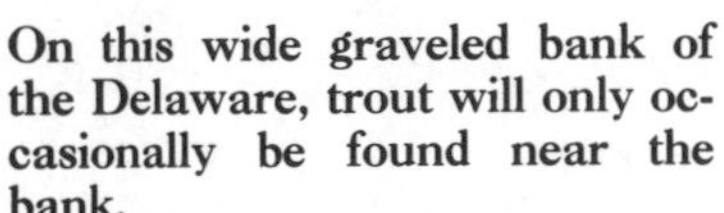

On this wide graveled bank of the Delaware, trout will only occasionally be found near the bank.

The line of bubbles along this bank means there is a steady supply of food there.

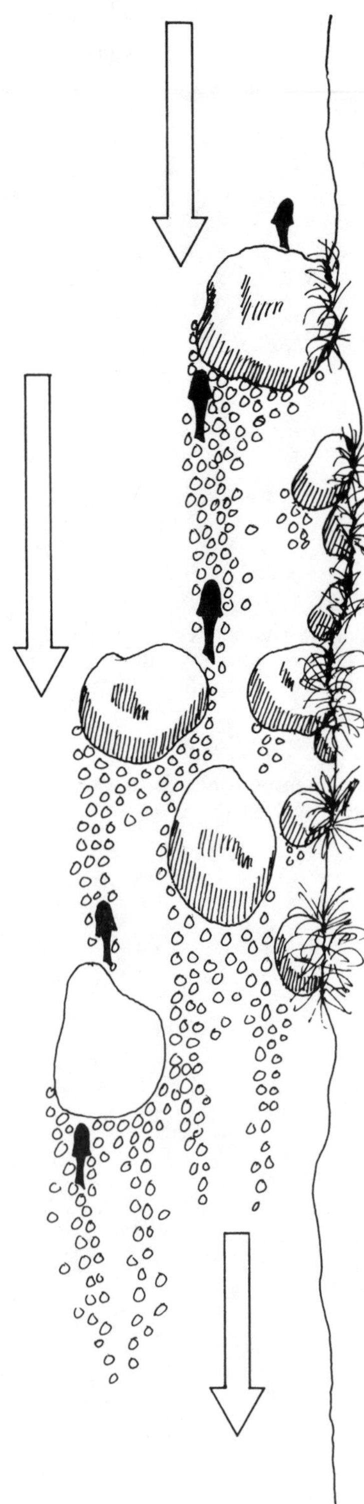

Where there is water of moderate depth and speed along a rocky bank, the trout will be found on the outside edges of the turbulence formed below the rocks, so the trout have access to a constant food supply.

rocks in these rivers to create white water or pocket water. Even the turbulent areas look smooth. And in both of these rivers, the most trout and the largest trout will be found along the banks, because this is the best place to find that one-half-foot-per-second current while still being within striking range of a steady food supply and shelter from predators.

The banks on the Railroad Ranch must be especially attractive because of the large number of ospreys that soar along the river, looking for easy targets. Where there are no big objects to protect a trout in midstream, a bank that is undercut is a haven from birds of prey. Fishermen stomp up and down the banks all day long, but if a trout is frightened away from its bank it will return within a half hour. Fishermen must be less of a threat than the birds.

You'll see fishermen poke their rods into undercut banks to see how far back they go, often exclaiming, "That hole goes back five feet—must be twenty trout in there." It's a hard theory to prove or disprove, but I've never seen a five-foot undercut produce more trout than a one-foot undercut. Think about it: all a trout needs for shelter from predators above, like ospreys and herons, is a foot anyway, and swimming predators, like otters or pike, would probably have the advantage in a dark hole. And what would a trout eat, five feet in from the edge of a current? Moles?

Banks don't have to be undercut to furnish protection from predators and the current. A jumble of big boulders along the bank can be one of the most productive spots for trout fishing. The Beaverkill and the lower Madison have good holding water for trout throughout a cross section of river, but where you find big rocks along the bank, combined with at least a part of main current, you'll find good trout and lots of them. You'll find most of the fish on the sides of the rocks adjacent to the main current, either in the cushion in front of, or the focal point behind the rocks. The sides of the rocks facing away from the main current are often quite sterile; there won't be much food here unless a thread of the main current winds around the sides closest to the bank.

A bank may appear to be completely smooth, with no cover for trout, even though the main current flows tight up against it. Look closely. Even the smallest promontory, just a six-inch finger of land jutting into the current, may be enough to attract a trout. One of my favorite pools on the East Branch of the Delaware River has held a nice trout for years. In the middle of a long, smooth bank is a finger of land that is no longer than your pinky. But just off the end of this little point, there is always a fat brown that dimples for spent caddis the whole month of May. If I hadn't seen a trout rising there I would never even have noticed the point, but since then I look for the spot each season and a large trout has always been there. I worry that some spring a flood will carve it away and then I'll have to start reading the water instead of lazily homing in on this spot.

Many animals prey on trout when they're young, but the list narrows as trout get big enough to be of interest to a fisherman. Most of their enemies attack from above. You can see how unconcerned trout are with large animals underwater if you snorkel a trout stream. They get a little nervous, they may stop rising, but they seldom flee unless you get within a few feet—and these are trout that wouldn't tolerate your presence

In a river like the Battenkill, with steep, densely vegetated banks, the trout may be concentrated near shore.

The Henry's Fork looks nothing like the Battenkill but the banks are still the most important place for the trout.

Tree roots and a steep slope usually indicate an undercut bank.

above the water thirty feet away. Otters are not common animals in many streams, nor are pike or water snakes large enough to eat a twelve-inch trout. Herons, ospreys, kingfishers, and mergansers are the major predators of adult trout, and all of them attack from above.

Along the banks, trout will choose places that are protected from above, if they have a choice. Some will be out in the open, but if there is a bush or tree hanging with its branches close to the water there will be a trout close by. Altitude is important—a tall dead tree with bare limbs overhanging the water will detract from the holding potential near that tree, because it's a great place for a kingfisher to perch and observe the river below. Where trees or bushes hang just a foot or two over the water, none of the food supply is strained away, yet the trout are still protected from above. Trout can be anywhere under the overhang, so you have to look for other clues within the sanctuary, like rocks or points of land.

Overhead cover can be an object that looks insubstantial to us. You see vivid examples of this in tiny meadow streams, like a spring creek tributary of the Snake River that harbors a population of large cutthroats. The eagles and ospreys are well aware of these trout, and eat a lot of them because the stream is shallow, clear, and devoid of large rocks and bank cover. At the upper end of the creek is a barbed-wire fence, three single strands that divide private property and BLM land. Yet there are sometimes half a dozen cutthroats over three pounds directly under the wire,

Trees like these two, with high bare branches that might be observation posts for a kingfisher, may mean that you'll find fewer trout under them than the water might indicate.

The three strands of barbed wire above this fisherman are enough protection to harbor four-pound trout in this tiny stream.

as those flimsy wires are enough to foil the attempts of even the most efficient bird of prey. And if you want to pick up a dozen Pale Morning Dun thorax flies in size 18, I've left enough of them swinging from those wires to last you a season.

Among the varieties of trees and shrubs that grow along banks, some attract more trout than others. Ordinary grasses and weeds at the edge of the stream don't provide substantial cover and aren't solid enough to change the course of a river when they grow close to it. Alders and similar shrubs, however, sprawl along the bank in all directions. Alders will root in the margins of streams and branches will extend up to several feet over the surface of the water. The phrase "alder-lined tunnel" is an overworked cliché used to describe small brook trout steams—but it's accurate.

Although alders themselves don't break the current substantially, they allow trout to live up against a bank, where the current is slower, with little fear of predation. Along an alder-lined bank, surface foods twirl along barely kissing the alder banks, and trout just poke their noses out from under the tangle for a meal.

Because alder and other streamside shrubs provide such valuable protection for trout, you may find nice trout tight to a bank in very shallow water. Several times in a row I spooked a brown trout of around fifteen inches in a spot where I normally waded carefully up the bank, casting to the center current, which featured an inviting rubble of grapefruit-sized rocks. I'd make a note in my diary to cast straight up along the alders the next time. Then I'd forget and spook him again. One afternoon he betrayed his position, rising to spent caddisflies, six inches from the bank, in water that was only eight inches deep for fifty feet upstream and down. I hooked him and he bolted into the alders, leapt over a tangle of branches inside, and broke my tippet.

All other things being equal, a bank that has only a small patch of alders growing in one spot will probably offer its best trout from beside that alder patch.

Trees growing close enough to the bank to poke their root systems into the water are a beacon to experienced trout fishermen. The roots provide an escape hatch; and the branches above, if they're close to the water, also keep away diving birds. The roots break the current; projecting out into the river, if only for a few inches, they make a dead spot. Often large tree roots are exposed where the main current tumbles against a bank, because the bank erodes until the water reaches something as solid as a tree. For generations, willows have been planted along trout streams because they thrive in wet areas and provide bank stabilization, shade, and places for trout to live. Willows are sometimes criticized because, not being strong trees, they can sometimes be blasted away by a flood—leaving a gaping hole in the stream bank. But I think their benefits far outweigh their drawbacks.

Willows also offer a secondary benefit to trout, more than any other tree. They weep. Wherever a willow branch touches the water or comes very close, you'll find a likely place for a trout. Those close branches keep away diving birds as surely as an undercut bank. Investigate each

A patch of alders makes this part of the bank even more attractive to trout.

With the trunk cut away, you can see the nice depression formed behind these roots.

one of them. If a willow grows three scraggly branches that hang just above the water, make a dozen casts to each place.

I spent my teenage years haunting a very productive limestone stream in upstate New York. One stretch of this river was nothing more than a half mile of featureless riffle, punctuated by four willow trees. But each tree was a pool in itself, with a trout hierarchy built around the tree—best trout just in front of the trunk (always the hardest spot to place a fly), second-best fish below the trunk, next biggest fish under the widest branch that grew close to the water, and so on down the line. Between the willows you'd catch only yearlings and young-of-the-year trout.

Weeds

When you approach a stream with heavy weed growth you throw away everything you've learned on tumbling, rocky rivers, or at least bend many of the rules. Trout in weed-filled waters have different behavior patterns, not so much because of the weeds themselves but because of the environment they indicate. Rooted aquatic weeds like watercress or *Ranunculus* need silt or mud to take hold, they need slower current to keep from getting ripped away, and, most important, they need stability. Periodic floods that scar and scour the bottom never let plant roots take hold long enough to establish expansive beds.

This stable, slow-moving environment is also richer because there is more primary production by the plants in the river bed. The insects that live here don't have to depend on outside sources of nutrients, like grasses and leaves falling into the river. The slow current produces an environment somewhere between a lake and a freestone river, and often the trout move, not from one discrete spot to another but they actually cruise around feeding, much like elk grazing in a meadow. And even a backwater tucked far away from the main current can offer enough food for a trout.

These slow, weedy, rich streams, called spring creeks in this country and chalkstreams in Europe, are rare jewels that receive attention disproportionate to their abundance because they produce many trout and large individuals. Reading a stream is not as essential on spring creeks because the trout can be anywhere. I've seen large brown trout on Pennsylvania's Letort Spring Run rising over muddy, shallow backwaters that offered absolutely no cover or any other advantage that I could tell. There is drifting food everywhere, and a stagnant backwater offers food plucked off the main current, yet lets trout hover below the surface without taxing their energy. You "read" the river here, for fly-fishing purposes, by looking for rising fish.

In fact, on most of the English trout streams the rules of the landowner or of the syndicate that controls the fishing rights prohibit "fishing the water," or casting blindly to a fish that has not been spotted. This makes more sense than at first appears to upstart Americans. Because these chalkstreams are clear and slow, the trout can spot you from a long distance away. For every unseen trout that you might present your fly prop-

Trout can be *anywhere* in a spring creek.

erly to, you will likely spook half a dozen others. And because the current is so slow, it is tough to cover a lot of water because ten seconds of drift on a chalkstream covers a lot less water than the same length of drift on a freestone river. Luckily, on this kind of river trout are almost always visible, either nymphing or rising to hatches of insects.

In this country rules are more lax, but whether you choose to fish only to visible fish or want to fish a spring creek blind, an education in reading the river can help. A weighted nymph fished in the deep channel between weed beds can be efficient, as can (gulp) a small Woolly Bugger, as a friend who regularly fishes a famous Montana spring creek confessed to me recently.

Gauge the places you look for trout in a spring creek by the current. Near the center of the stream, where the current is at its fastest, trout will lie behind, in front of, and to the sides of weed beds, because they still need some relief from the current. On weeds that are completely submerged, a favorite spot is on top of the leading edge of a weed bed, where there is a cushion of slower water and an unobstructed view of drifting food. Unlike rocks, weed beds are food producers, and one clump of weeds will hold thousands of freshwater crustaceans like sow bugs and scuds, plus many species of swimming mayfly nymphs. Thus you might find trout directly in the lee of weed beds, waiting for goodies to be dislodged.

Extensive weed growth will split the current into channels, and deep alleys between weeds are sometimes the only place the trout have to live.

In spring creeks, look for channels between weed beds. Note the trout rising in the channel.

Where you have a weed bed that borders the main current on one side and a backwater on the other, the trout will be more likely to lie on the side adjacent to the main current. I've asked spring creek fishermen from as far away as England and Argentina where they find the most fish, and after a little head scratching the answer is usually "on the current side of shoreline weeds."

Deep pools are rare in spring creeks, and are often surprisingly unproductive where they do occur. Spring creeks have so much food and such extensive cover in the form of weed beds that the easiest place for a trout to live is in a "flat," in only a foot or two of water. I once spent a single afternoon on a delightful little English chalkstream named the Derbyshire Wye. Scattered among long stretches of shallow gravel runs striped with weed beds were a few deep, tree-lined bend pools that were well over waist deep. A heavy hatch had started of Pale Wateries—a mayfly similar to our Pale Evening Dun in size, color, and behavior. I saw many good trout rising in the shallow channels, and after catching a few moved upstream to one of the deep pools. Then I took a look at one of the deep pools downstream. Both contained only a couple of small fry, and when I returned to the shallow flats they were still full of decent trout rising.

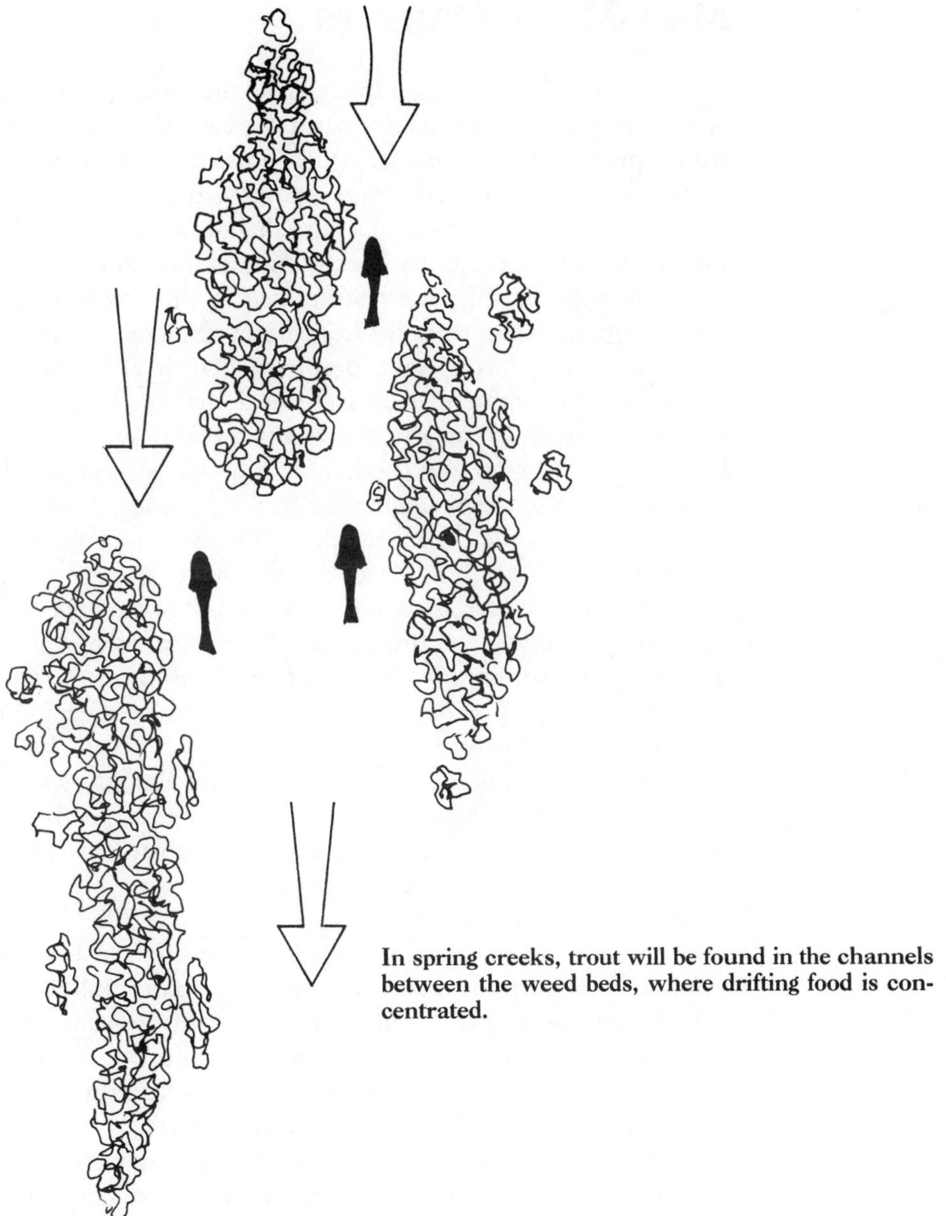

In spring creeks, trout will be found in the channels between the weed beds, where drifting food is concentrated.

Similarly, the occasional fast riffle in a spring creek may disappoint you. At the tail of the famous Ginger Beer stretch of the Test in southern England is a beautiful stretch of what we would call pocket water. The rest of this stretch is flat, slow water. When I asked my English friends if I could try the fast water, they shrugged and said all right, if I really wanted to, using much the same tone as they would to a young boy who wants to skip stones while his father fishes. After a half hour, I sheepishly made my way upstream, where they were into dozens of rising trout. I hadn't seen a single fish below.

I've repeated this performance in several spring creeks in Montana and Wyoming, always ignoring the advice of people who fish the streams day after day. But I should know better—why would a trout fight the current when he can drop downstream fifty yards and get the same amount of food in a leisurely current?

MAN-MADE OBJECTS

With rare exception, man-made structures or deposits in a river are less attractive to trout than nearby natural areas. Man loves straight lines and nature prefers smooth curves, which provide more nooks and crannies for protecting trout from a current. Generally, the only way man can improve on a stretch of river is to take a flat, shallow area and provide more places for a trout to live, either by constricting its flow so that depth is increased or by *carefully* placing *proper* structures in the water. A poorly designed "stream improvement" will often direct the flow of the current into an erodable bank, causing more problems than it alleviates.

The worst example of man's physical changes to a river is channelization. The stream is straight, the banks are high and piled with rock, and little vegetation grows on the banks. The purpose of channelization is to prevent the water from dissipating any of its energy here, and to move it downstream as quickly as possible. The result is little turbulence, no slower pockets, and few places for a trout to escape the ravages of the current. Channelized areas are often diked with rock that comes from non-riverine sources, so the edges of the rocks along the bank are sharp and spiny. Trout prefer to lie next to and on top of the smooth, rounded rocks that currents sculpt so even the banks of a channelized river are barren and inhospitable.

Such water is generally worthless, so you should avoid it. Seldom are entire rivers channelized, and if given the choice of fishing upstream or downstream of a channelized area I'd go upstream. Downstream, silt, gravel, and sand from the channelization are carried by the current, filling in pools and suffocating young trout and insect life.

Channelized areas can come back to life but this can take decades. A wonderful brook trout feeder stream of the Battenkill was channelized in a fit of hysteria following a flood, to save a private campground. That was in 1973. Today, there are a couple of pools and a few trout have returned, but the scars remain. It will be fifty years before this area is again prime trout water—longer if it is channelized again.

Riprapping or cribbing may look like channelization on a small scale but its use is usually beneficial to the trout. Here, material is placed along a bank to keep it from eroding. Instead of a shallow, silty, eroded area with no cover you get a deeper bank with some irregular surfaces that cause turbulence. Cribbing can be large rocks dumped onto the bank or carefully anchored logs covered with chicken wire and with the spaces between the logs filled with gravel. Rock cribbing may not be attractive to trout for several years because the sharp edges of the rocks need to be smoothed and the settling of unstable rocks may frighten the trout away. When you look at rock-cribbed areas look for signs that the rock below the surface has been smoothed. If it has been there for a year or so it will probably be covered by a layer of algae and diatoms; this makes the rock look dirty. Clean-looking cribbing that looks freshly dumped will have no vegetation growing in or around it.

When log cribbing is placed along a bank, fishery managers will often extend the surface of the cribbing a foot or two out over the water, making secure places for trout to hide. They can also be tough places to fish.

A channelized area. It will be decades before a trout of any size lives here.

This trout has moved out from under the log cribbing on the bank to feed.

Extensive work on Wiscoy Creek in upstate New York, with beautiful undercut cribbing, produced trout that would only venture out beyond the cribbing when a heavy hatch was in progress. The fish grew larger but got much more difficult to catch.

Fish will be found all along log cribbing, especially where there is a bush or tree that hangs over the cribbing for additional shelter. Since it is man-made and pretty straight, trout can be holding anywhere along the length. Just make sure that a primary current is bringing food to the cribbing, or the most promising undercut will be barren. There is some beautiful cribbing on a big pool in the trophy area of the Battenkill in New York State, but it's in a backwater, and the primary current flows to the other side of the river. I've never seen a trout feed near this cribbing.

Deflectors are structures designed not to harbor trout but to narrow the current, deepen it, or direct it to the far bank. A well-designed deflector

The best fishing might be found on the bank opposite this deflector.

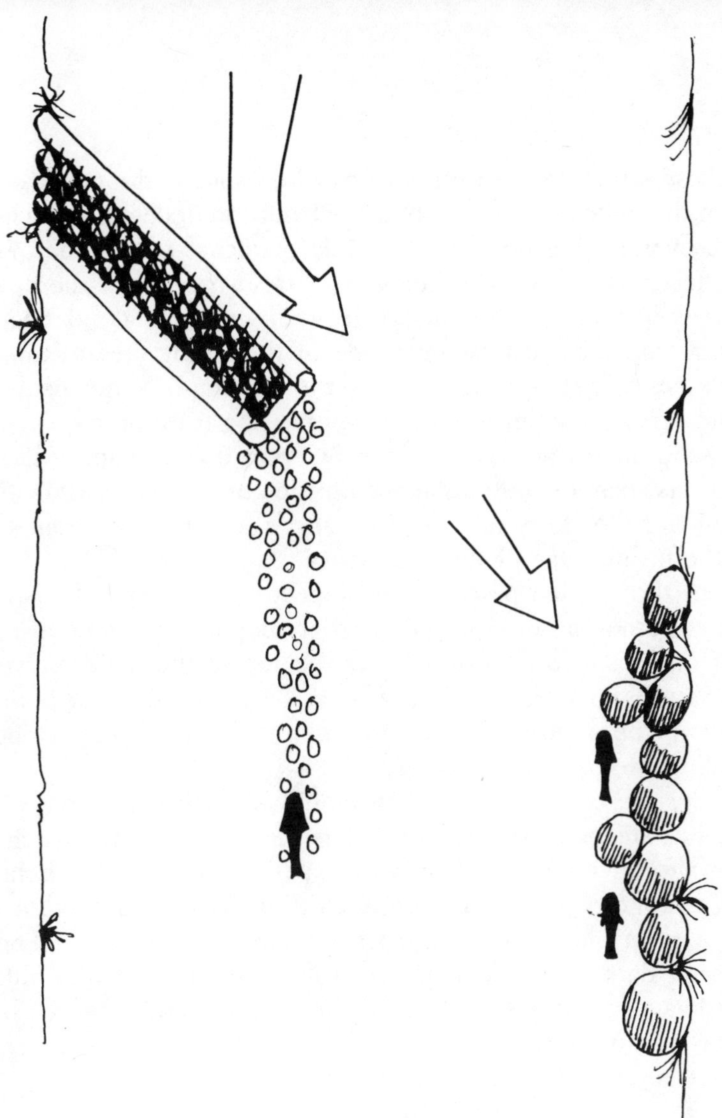

Trout may be found in the seam below a deflector—but don't neglect the opposite bank.

does not work at high water—in flood, the water will pass over the top of a deflector. It's in the low water of midsummer that a deflector becomes valuable, turning a shallow, exposed flat into a deeper channel that provides more cover for the trout and keeps the water moving before it warms up too much.

When you see a deflector you should direct your attention to the place the water is being deflected *to,* not to the deflector. First, somebody thought that the bank opposite the deflector, or the main channel, had more value than the shallow bank the deflector was located on. Second, deflectors are built as smooth as possible, to discourage turbulence, so there won't be many little nooks of dead spots around its surface. Third, the area behind a deflector usually silts in fairly quickly, leaving a relatively barren spot for trout habitat. And fourth, every fisherman in the world has to walk out to the end of a deflector before he starts fishing, guaranteeing that any fish that lived there would soon move out in fright.

During high water, or in streams that have flows around the deflectors that are deep enough—say over two feet deep—you may find some fish around these structures. An often-overlooked spot is the crook or elbow in front of the deflector, especially if the bank the deflector is anchored to has some overhanging brush or a jumble of rocks. In an older, broken-down deflector that has some holes in it, trout may sit in the dead spot immediately in front of the deflector. In the eddy behind a deflector, the prime spot would be just to the inside of the strong area of turbulence that trails below the outside edge of the deflector. Some fish may lie tucked in under the point of the deflector, using it for protection as well, but I've seen more trout lying four or five feet downstream of the point. A deflector is such a strong influence on the current that turbulence may be carried thirty or forty feet downstream, again with the trout hanging just on the inside edge of the turbulence.

Between the outside point of the deflector and the bank, below the deflector, whether or not trout will be there depends on the height of the water. If there is water breaking over the top of the deflector you may find a trout. If no water is coming over the top, the water behind the deflector will be almost stagnant and won't provide enough food for a drift-feeding trout.

But there are two instances that should prompt you to look a little closer at this stagnant backwater. One is just after a heavy hatch, when the main current might be cleared of mayflies but the eddy behind the deflector is a merry-go-round of crippled flies that didn't make it off the surface. A trout may cruise into here for some easy dessert. The other time is after dark. The stagnant backwater, because it won't hold trout under ordinary conditions, is a haven for minnows and crayfish. Large—very large—trout will cruise into these spots after dark, when they have the advantage over their quicker prey.

Bridges are our keyholes into a trout's world, where we park our cars and look for them. Do bridges offer anything special? We hear stories about the giant trout that lives under the Mill Street bridge, but is this because the Mill Street bridge is the only place we can look into the water?

A bridge's value seems to be directly related to its size and height. The smaller and lower the bridge, the more likely the bridge structure itself will attract trout. Here, for simplicity's sake, I am ignoring everything else in the river bed, save what actual value the bridge provides.

Goddard and Clarke, in their thought-provoking English book *The Trout and the Fly*, put high value on bridges for attracting trout. This seemed contrary to what I'd observed in this country until I saw a picture of the bridges they were talking about—low footbridges, with barely a foot of clearance between the water and the bridge. Such bridges provide protection for a trout, giving no vantage point to a heron or osprey, and with no shunting off of the food supply in the current.

Contrast this to the Route 17 highway bridge over the Beaverkill at the head of Cairn's Pool, where hundreds of fishermen each week cast delicately tied Hendricksons to the tune of eighteen-wheelers thundering hundreds of feet overhead. Other than aesthetics, does this bridge add anything? The concrete pylons, anchored in the center of the river, are smooth, designed to create as little turbulence as possible, so the

This covered bridge may be picturesque but I doubt if the trout care. ***Photo by Margot Page.***

cushions ahead and dead spots below are small. Of course the bridge provides some shade, but trout don't need shade that doesn't provide cover, and what good is cover if it's the length of a long pool above?

In between is the typical secondary-highway bridge, with a well-worn path to the river. Is this pool worthy of any special attention? It might be deep and dark, and there may be a monster there—but every other fisherman who has ever passed through has tried for him. Unless you see something interesting in a particular bridge pool, I recommend that you pass them up.

4
Pools

Pools are places where the current slows, deepens, and, most often, widens. A pool can be two or 200 feet wide. What we would call a major pool in a tiny mountain brook would only be a small pocket in a large river—it could hold just as many trout in the big river but it might go unnoticed. To differentiate between pools and pockets, a pocket holds just a part of a river's current, but a pool occupies a river's entire flow, from bank to bank.

Water flows in at the head of a pool. The center of the current where the water first breaks over is the throat, the fastest current in the pool. The throat soon flattens and spreads out to form the tongue. At either side of the tongue and throat are seams, or eyes as they call them in New Zealand, where the current is considerably slower. If the current is fast enough, the exchange of water between the seams and the main current will exhibit some centrifugal force and form a whirlpool, where the water immediately next to the bank will run "backward" or upstream.

As the tongue widens, turbulence lessens, and the surface of the water flattens at the middle of the pool. You can still see the threads of main current flow, though, identified as lines of bubbles or debris. The main current thread may trail straight down the middle of the pool, it may swing toward either bank, or it may split. In large trout rivers like the Delaware on the border of New York and Pennsylvania, the pools are so large—half a mile or more—and the slope of the land so gentle that the

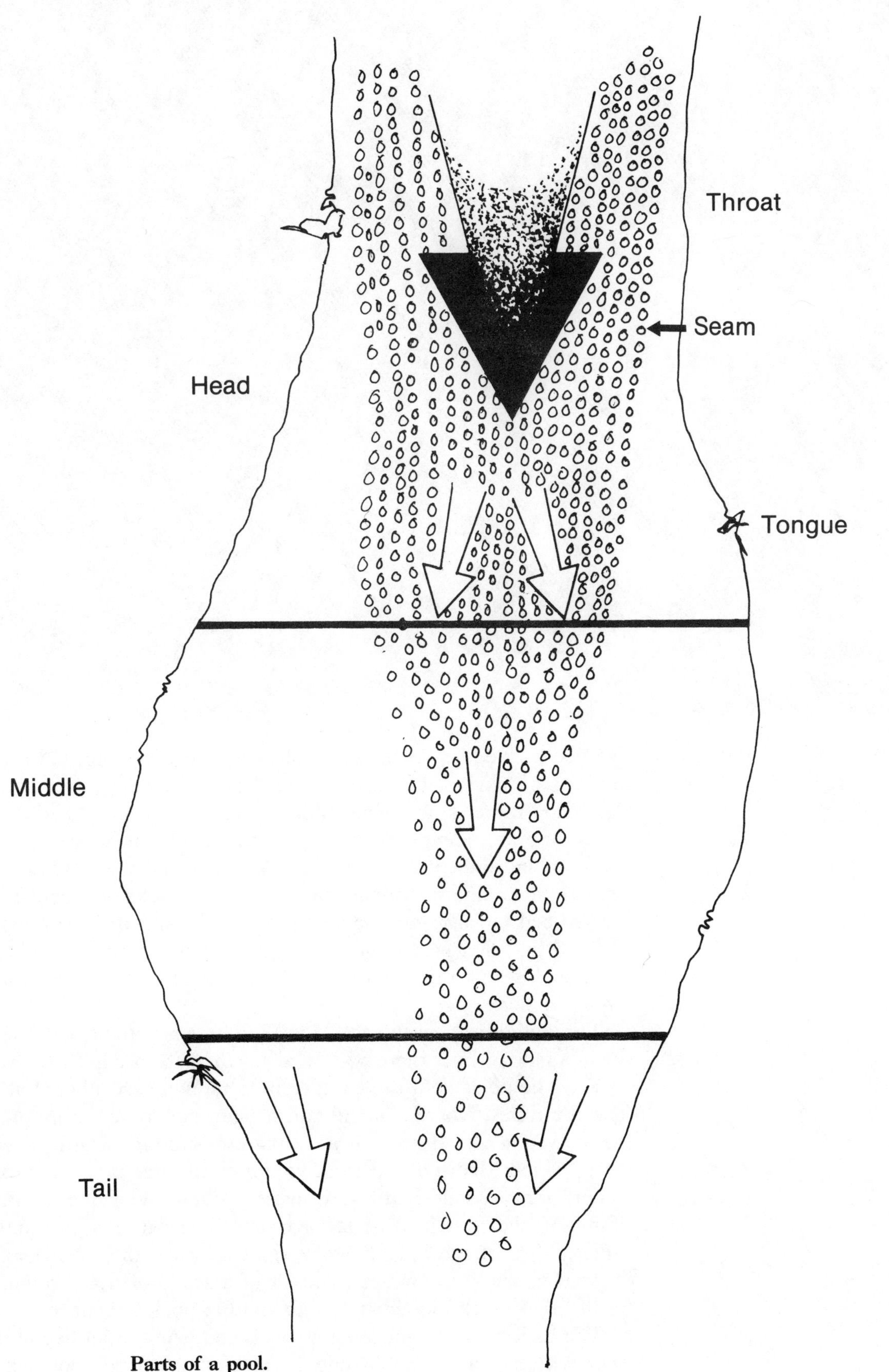

Parts of a pool.

A classic pool. The angler is fishing to the tongue.

big pools, or eddies as they are called on the Delaware, have the characteristics of lakes. The current thread is lost in the lower part of these pools and there is no visible turbulence.

As the water approaches the tail of the pool, the stream bed shallows, narrows, and the current begins to pick up speed again. Flow is normally smooth here, almost laminar, unless there are rocks or irregularities in the stream bed to cause turbulence. Then, in a rush, there is usually a well-defined line that marks the starting point for a riffle or the head of the next pool, where the water breaks into turbulence in response to a quickening in slope.

The optimum pool-to-riffle ratio in a stream is thought to be 1:1; that is, in a mile of river there will be as much space occupied by riffles as by pools. The pools hold the adult trout (although certainly not all of them) and the riffles, where sunlight and oxygen penetrate, easily produce and harbor young fish. But this is not a prerequisite for a healthy trout stream. Parts of the Madison and the Deschutes in Oregon are unbroken riffle water for many miles, and slow-floating, stable rivers like the Fall in California or the Bow in Alberta have extensive flats that are unbroken by riffles. Most of the upland brook trout rivers of the Appalachians, from New Hampshire to Georgia, consist of a series of deep, round "plunge pools" that break immediately into another pool without forming a riffle.

The easiest way to get to know pools and where trout live in them is to start with a stylized pool—one I call a symmetrical pool, with a well-defined head and tail, and a slow middle. In such a pool, the main current runs down the center with a well-defined seam at each side of the head.

The Throat

At the throat of the pool, water rushes in quickly, and because of the force of that current, rocks, logs, and other obstructions are gradually pushed aside. Only the largest boulders and pieces of bedrock remain standing against the flow. The throat is one of the places in a pool that gets the most attention from fishermen, but it's one of the least likely places to find trout, especially larger ones. Because the throat has usually swept away all obstructions, a trout would have to fight the current constantly. Unless there are obvious signs of a large obstruction in the throat—bumps or turbulence—it may be a waste of time to cast your fly at this spot, except if you're placing your fly here to get a good drift in the place where the throat changes into the tongue.

The other situation where you would find trout right in the throat of a pool would be in a river where the gradient is slight, forming just a gentle riffle in the head of the pool. If there are no standing waves at the head of a pool, and the force of the current is spread out over a wide area instead of a narrow slot, trout will be found scattered throughout the head of the pool, concentrated where there are rocks or depressions in the stream bed.

The Tongue and Seams

As the throat roars into a pool and forms the tongue, it begins to tumble and form standing waves. Invariably there will be an underwater shelf, unless the stream bed is composed of hard bedrock. Just under the lip of this shelf is an area of calm water where the velocity is nearly zero, yet a fish lying here has easy access to the food line above. The best part of this shelf is the first few feet, because downstream of that point the calm water begins to mix with the faster water above and the turbulence can be violent enough to be uncomfortable for trout. You can spot the upstream edge of the shelf by looking for two things: either the point in the tongue where standing waves begin to form or, if the water is clear, you'll see a distinct line where the color of the water darkens, changing from a tan to a deep brown, or from pale green to deep blue, depending on the color of the water and the stream bed.

This traditional "hot spot" is not as productive as you may have read. When snorkeling rivers, I've looked at this tumbling, bubbly world many times and never seen a really large trout under the lip of a shelf. It is usually occupied by small or medium-sized rainbows or brook trout. Big trout, if they are to be found at the head of the pool, are more likely to be found in the slower seams at either side of the throat.

The throat and tongue at the head of a pool. The throat is at A, the tongue at B. Here you might find trout behind the submerged rock at C or, in times of high water, in the backwater at D.

The shelf at the head of this pool is clearly defined by the change of the bottom from light to dark.

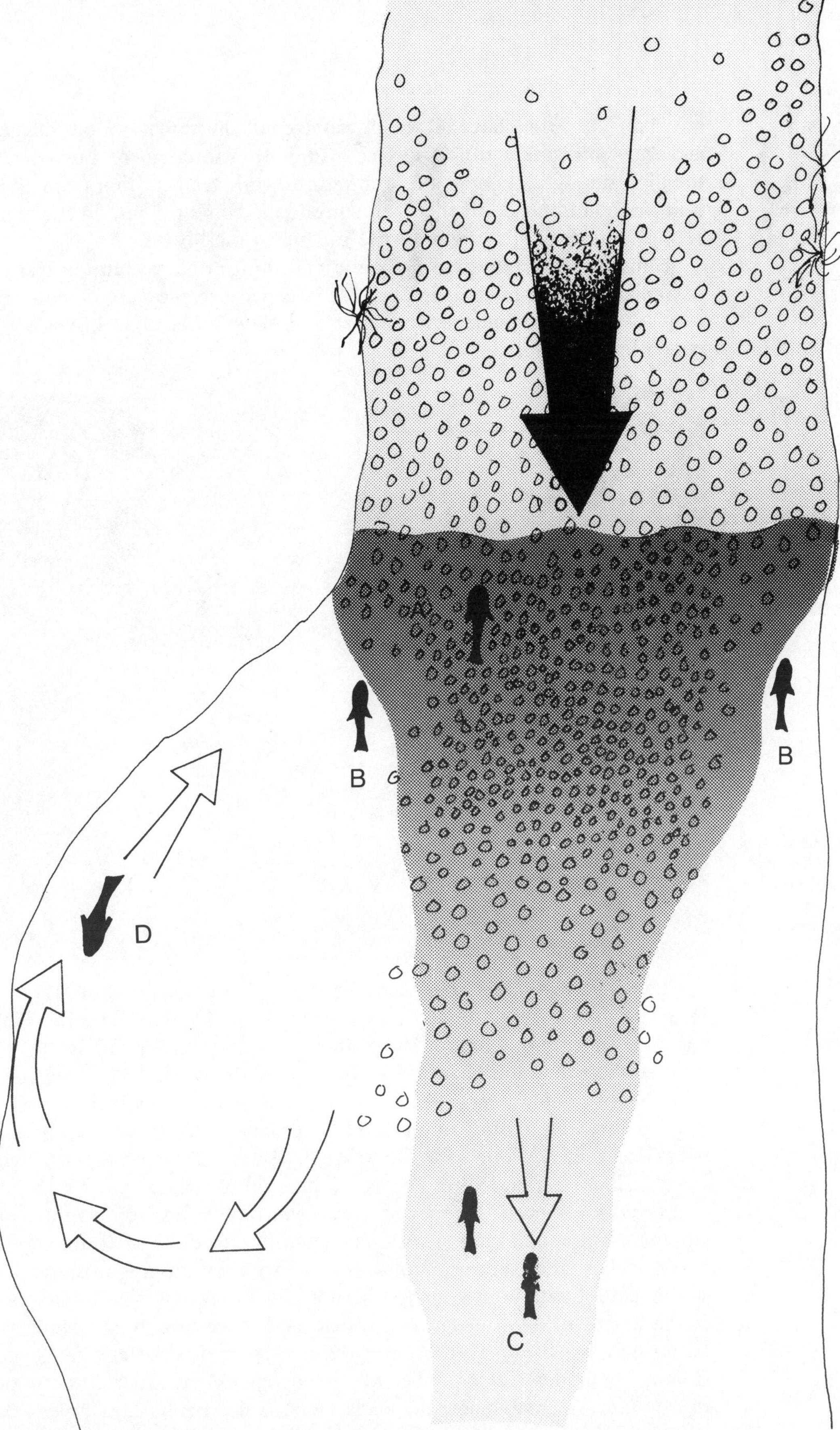

Lies at the head of a pool. The fish at A is lying just below the shelf where the pool deepens quickly. The two trout at B are in the seam along the side of the throat, and the two fish at C are in the tongue. The trout at D is in a whirlpool and faces downstream.

Why? The seams have all the advantages of the throat—food, oxygen, and the protection a riffled surface affords from predators—but none of the disadvantages, namely a fast current to work against. Trout can either wait for food to break off the main current and come to them in the seam, or they can drift sideways into the tongue to pick it off.

Seams are almost always one of the first things trout fishermen learn to recognize because of their importance and because they are obvious and easy to spot. The line between fast and slow water is as distinct as a pencil line on paper.

A clear example of a seam, just out from the bank on the right side of the photo. Seams on the inside of a bend, as this one is, may often hold the best trout in a pool.

I had underestimated the value of these seams until fishing the Big Hole one July with guide and lodge owner Dave Decker. The Big Hole has a classic riffle-pool ratio; the bottom is mainly gravel and small cobbles, so the riffles and heads of pools are smooth and devoid of the cover a jumble of boulders might offer. The seams of these pools didn't seem to have anything to offer to big trout. Yet many of them gave up browns over sixteen inches long to an Olive Woolly Bugger. Since then I've given even shallow, barren-looking seams a thorough workout.

If the throat current is very fast, it can whirl the seams around and form whirlpools on one or both sides. Look carefully for them by watching the bubbles along the bank next to the seam. Are they running upstream? If so, be careful with both your approach and your casting. You'll find trout facing upstream right next to the throat, and those next to the bank will be facing downstream. In between the two is an almost stagnant "eye." Coming from downstream, you might not spook the trout next to the throat but you may spook the ones next to the bank. And unless the whirlpool is large, it's hard to fish a dry fly because your line and leader invariably fall across two or three currents at once, immediately dragging the fly.

I guess that's why those Woolly Buggers work so well in the seam—you just slap them in and begin stripping, so drag isn't a factor.

In a whirlpool, trout seem to prefer the predictable current at either side of the "eye" to swirling water in the center. The sides of the whirlpool carry more food because they're more in touch with the main current. If you watch the center of a whirlpool you'll notice that mayflies or debris trapped there whirl around and around. A trout waiting there for insects might be able to capture them easily but he wouldn't have access to as many in the course of a day as he would on the faster current at either side of the center.

Middle of the Pool

As the tongue of the current begins to slow down, the line between the tongue and the seam becomes less distinct. Here, in the middle of the pool, you come to the most productive part of a pool as far as numbers of trout are concerned—assuming the middle of the pool has sufficient depth to hold trout, at least two feet of water. Because of the slower current a trout doesn't need as large an obstruction for current protection as he would in the head so there are more trout per square foot. At the head of a raging pool, it might take a rock that is at least a foot in diameter to give sanctuary to a trout. In the middle of the pool he might need only a four-inch rock to keep him in place without wasting energy.

It is astounding how many trout these "flats" can hold, and you can't appreciate it until you see these areas either in the midst of a heavy spinner fall, when every trout in the river is rising, or during an electroshocking by a fisheries biologist. But the middle of a pool is often ignored. There are no obvious places, like at the head of a pool. If we don't see anything, we move on.

Don't. Take a closer look. First, find the main current threads, which should be visible as bubble lines. Then look for backwaters. Look at where the stream bed changes from a washed-clean look to a silt-covered color—this will vary depending on water chemistry and geology. Another way of looking for backwaters is to look where dead leaves and other debris collect at the edges of the stream.

Between the outside edge of backwater and the fastest water in the center of the pool is where you'll most likely find trout. If the water is moving fast, over five feet per second, look off to the side of the main current. There will usually be a distinct line dividing the fast water from the more comfortable water at the edges. The "good" water in a fast river, like the Bighorn in Montana, may extend right up to the bank with no backwaters to worry about. In fact, in rich rivers like the Bighorn the so-called "backwaters" carry enough food and have enough current that they are sometimes the best places to find trout.

This area of productive water in the middle of a pool often changes with water levels. In the early season or when the river is in flood, there may be standing waves all the way down the middle of the pool, like the

The middle of a pool. At first glance it seems as though the trout could be anywhere.

hairs standing up on the back of a dog's neck. Here you'll find the trout well out of the main current, as close to the banks as possible while still having access to some moving water.

As the water recedes, the area of comfortable water moves away from the bank and toward the center (in our hypothetical symmetrical pool where the fastest current runs down the middle of the pool), although the exact center may still be too fast. Later, in midsummer, the very center of the river where the main current-threads flow will be the only place in the middle of the pool that offers enough flow to maintain a steady supply of food.

Once you've identified where the trout will lie in relation to current speed, look for obstructions. Surface wrinkles. Swirls. Objects sticking out of the water. The kind of mid-pool bottom that holds the most amount of trout is a cobble bottom—a contiguous jumble of grapefruit to watermelon-sized rocks. It's also the hardest type of water to read, because the trout can be anywhere. Why a nice fourteen-inch brown will use one piece of granite for a pillow and not the one five feet away that looks exactly the same to you is a secret the trout will keep from us forever.

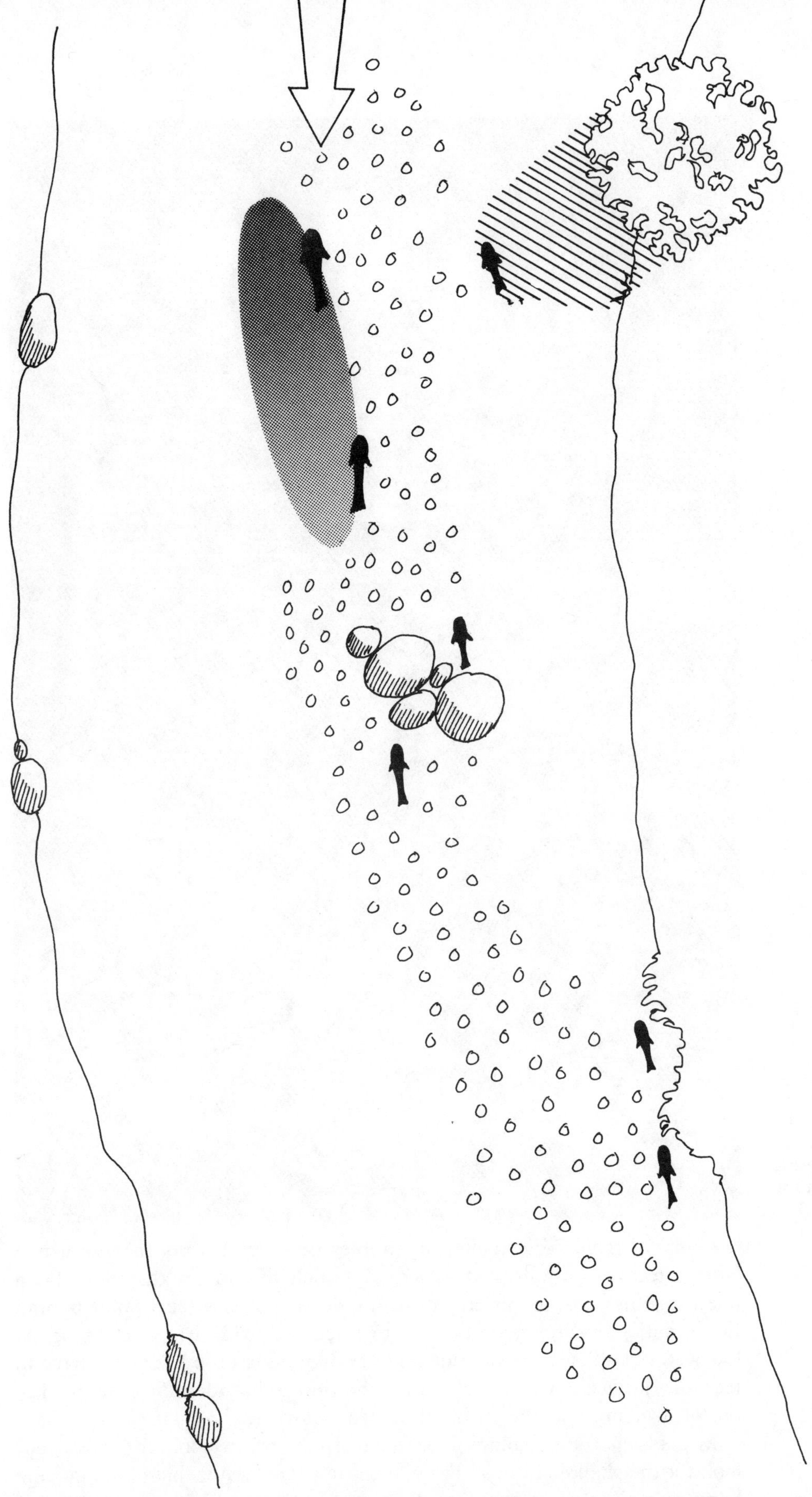

The middle of a pool may not be as devoid of trout as you think. Look for them in the shade of overhanging trees, especially in the outside edge of the shade (A), along the edge of deep cuts (B), near piles of cobbles (C), and along alders and other streamside brush where the bubble line of the current touches the bank (D).

In a deep pool with steep sides like this one on the Merced River in California, look for the shallowest places in the pool. My bet would be in front of the big rock in the foreground, or in the eddy behind it.

Look for the largest rocks, or jumbles of several rocks that form one larger piece of bottom obstruction. A bunch of cobbles that have been piled together by the current to form a dead spot and focal point behind them that is anywhere from a foot to three feet wide is a prime spot. At low water you'll see the obstructions; at higher water levels you'll have to read the surface current, looking for the bump that identifies the head of the obstruction and the turbulence just below it.

In pools that are shallow, look for deep spots. In pools that are deep, look for the shallow places. Trout seem to prefer water that is somewhere between six inches and six feet deep, to keep a practical balance between

In this shallow pool, most of the trout will be in the deep slot in the center of the pool, which shows up as a dark line. An especially productive spot would be the line where the shallows meet the deep slot in the foreground.

In an otherwise featureless pool, this tree will harbor half a dozen decent trout. The largest fish may be found right under the outside branches.

obtaining food and escaping from predators. A rainbow in a deep, dark pool with fjord-like banks will be attracted to a place where he can be near the surface and mid-water—where most of the drifting food is accessible. Shelves and gravel bars not only let him rest near the surface, they also form dead spots in the current that are just as nice as those made by rocks.

In a barren-looking pool that is barely a foot deep in places, look for channels or "cuts" that might be the only water deep enough to make a trout feel secure. These spots must be at least the size of a single bed if there is no other cover around that a trout can use for a bolt-hole. If a brown trout gets pinned down by a kingfisher in a slot that is two feet deep but only a couple of feet wide by four feet long, he's going to be eaten. On the other hand, if that same little slot is up against an undercut bank or a sunken log, it might be a place for a brown to grow smart, fat, and old.

Bars and cuts are tough to spot in the middle of a pool where there may not be enough current to form turbulence, especially in the early part of the season, when the water is too deep and dirty for you to see the bottom. Later in the year, using polarized sunglasses, look for changes in the color of the bottom. Lighter colors indicate shallower water; darker water than that surrounding a spot betrays a cut. Another way to spot changes in depth is to try to discern objects on the bottom. If you can pick out all the stones on the bottom except in one place where the bottom looks blurry, you've found a cut.

A large tree that stretches out over the pool may key you into other places. The shade cast by the tree will be a more likely spot for trout than the bright area beyond. The sages of trout fishing proclaim that trout, browns in particular, are uncomfortable in bright sunlight. I believe this is bunk for several reasons. First, large brown trout often *do* feed in bright sunlight, right out in the open. Second, the best feeding position in an area of shade, the place taken by the largest trout, is sometimes right at the narrow point of shade farthest from the bank, not in the larger patch of shade closest to the bank. Because trout don't have eyelids and can't squint, they can see better and have an advantage over their prey when *they* are in the shade and the prey drifts in from the sunlight. This also helps to explain why trout feed ravenously just after the sun leaves the water in the evening, even if the water temperature hasn't cooled a bit. They aren't blinded by the sun but insects are still well silhouetted against the twilight. And doesn't surface feeding often stop at complete darkness, even when there are still plenty of insects on the water?

Tail of the Pool

The tail of a pool is the most underfished, underestimated, and difficult part of a river. It is a prime place for large trout for a number of reasons. First, because the water is shallower and smoother here than anywhere else in the pool (generally), a trout can see everything that goes on above the water—both predators and food. Large trout do not grow old ignoring what happens on the surface and above it.

The tail of a pool is one of the toughest—and most worth-while—places to fish.

In a tail with few big rocks on the bottom and lush banks, the best trout will be found along the banks. A nice trout has just risen in front of the stick along the right bank.

In this tail, you would expect few trout near the far bank with the exception of the area around the rock; a better possibility is along the big rocks on the near bank, and also around the flat boulders in the center of the river.

Second, it is efficient for a trout to feed on drift here, because the narrowing of the stream both horizontally and vertically concentrates all the food that is drifting in the pool above.

Third, it's rough to catch these trout from above, because they can spot you easily when they're lying in thin water, and if you approach them from below, the water at your feet is always much faster than the water where your fly lands—drag is a problem the instant your fly hits the water.

And there are other reasons known only to the trout. But I've seen and caught more large trout in the tail, by a wide margin, than any other place in a pool. Big rivers and little brooks. East and West. Spring creeks and limestoners.

The stream bottom at the tail of a pool may slope upward gradually, or it may shallow abruptly, forming a deep bowl. If there is an abrupt change in depth, trout will be lined up along the spot where deep water turns shallow, as a distinct cushion will be formed here. A trout doesn't need a rock for protection here.

On the other hand, a tail that shallows gradually may hold trout almost anywhere. The Vs of submerged rocks will be easy to spot in this shallow water, which gives you some hints as to where the trout may be. Tails like this can be hundreds of feet wide and a quarter of a mile long, so anything that narrows down the search is helpful.

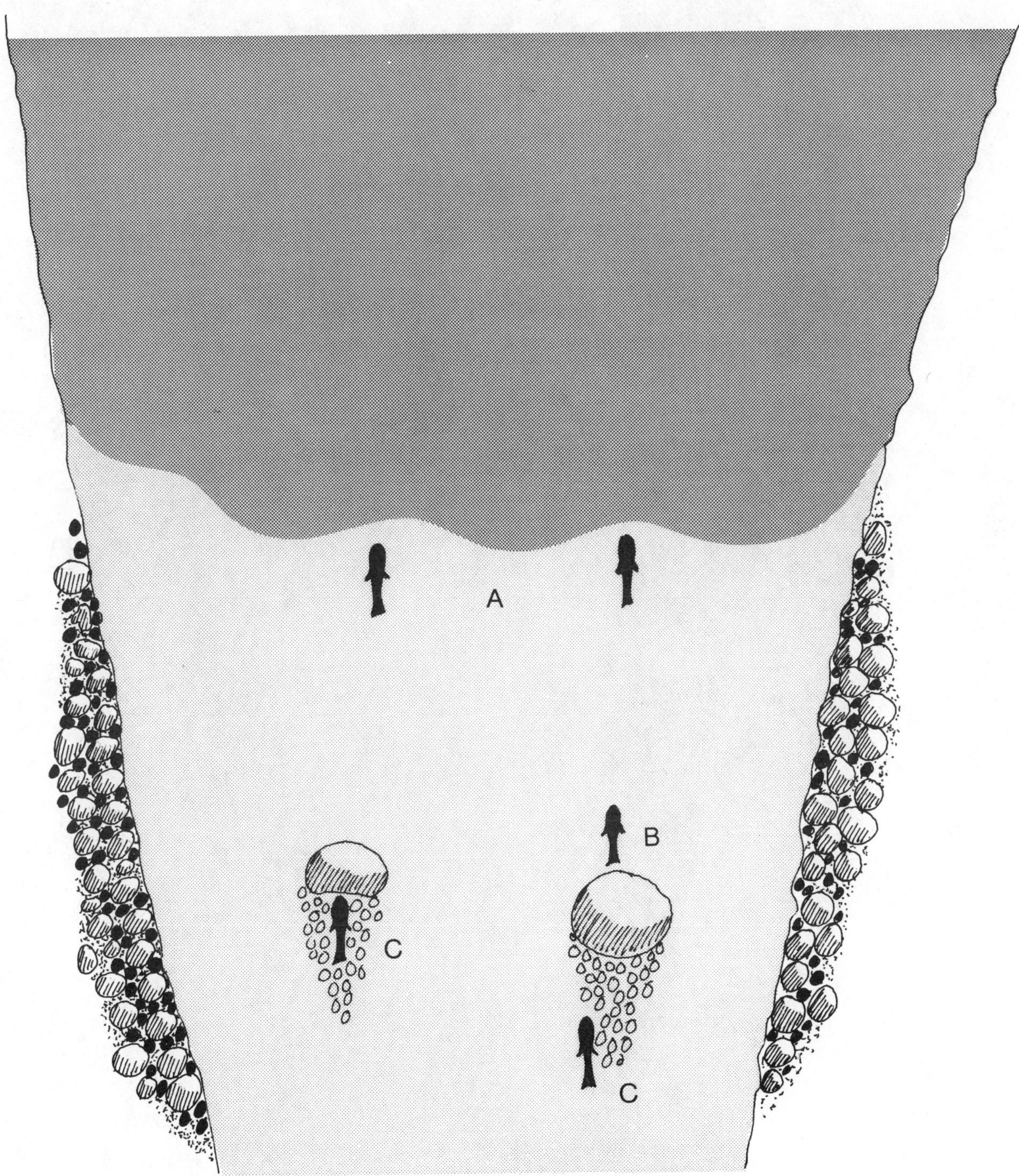

Lies in the tail of a pool with wide gravel banks. The trout at A are at the point where the pool shallows abruptly. The trout at B is in front of a rock in the shallow part of the tail; and the two trout at C are in the Vs behind the rocks.

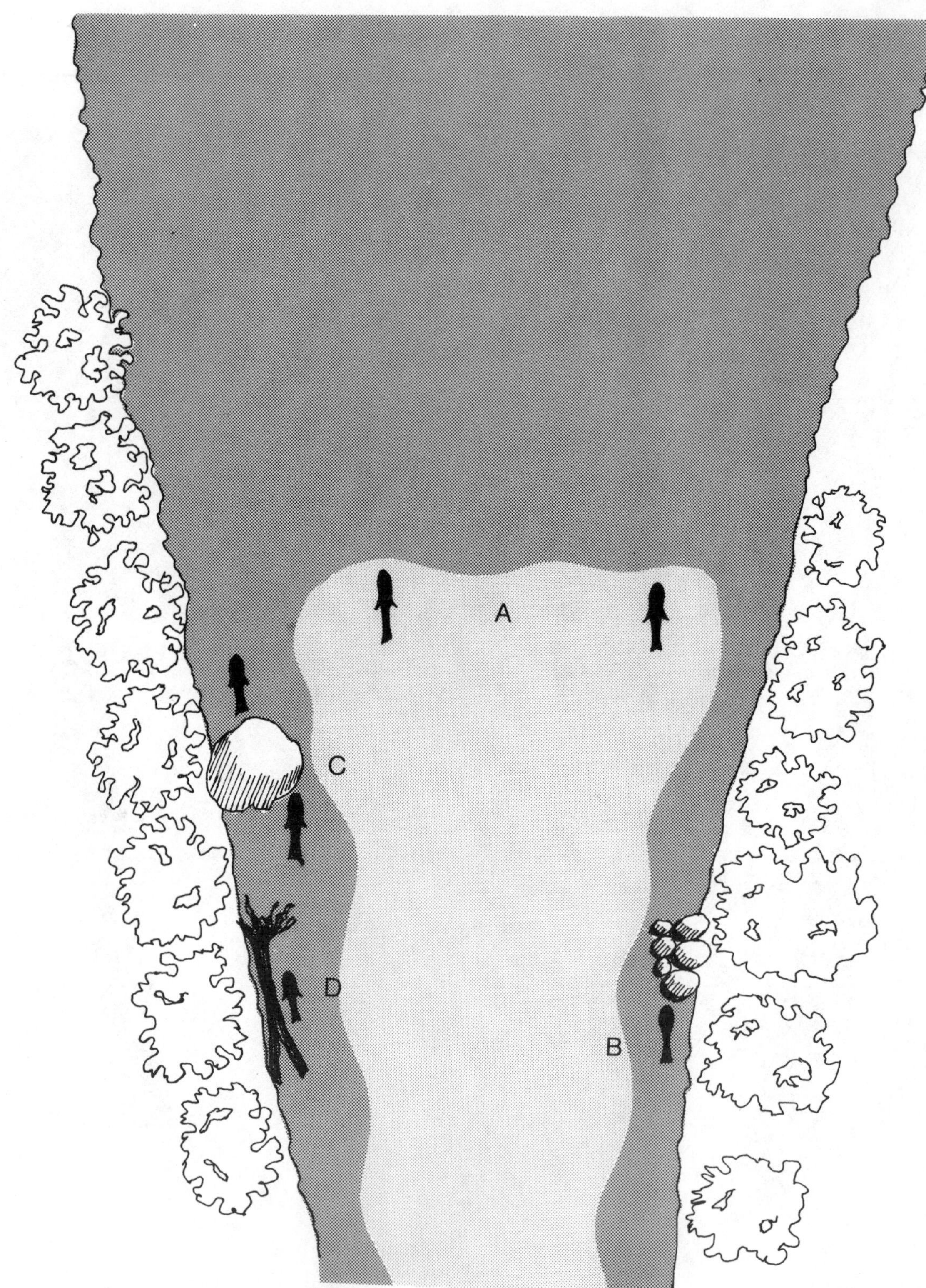

Lies in the tail of a pool with a shallow center and no big rocks on the bottom in the center of the river. The trout at A are on the shelf where the pool shallows. The trout at B is behind a pile of cobbles along the bank. The trout at C are in front of and behind a large rock on the bank. D is a fish lying along a partially submerged log.

In rivers with wide gravel banks, the trout are more likely to be found in the center of the river than near the banks. The water gets shallow near shore and there is nowhere to hide if danger looms. In rivers that have stable banks with vegetation, whether it is mature trees, alders, or grasses, the tail of a pool right up against the bank can be *the* number-one spot for large trout.

Banks with vegetation or tree roots on them are almost always deeper and more undercut than wide graveled banks. A little vegetation hanging or trailing over the water seems to make this spot even more appealing. You'll be amazed at how little depth is needed to hold a trout along the bank here—a foot of water will hold a fifteen-inch trout if he has a safe place to go when an osprey flies over.

Friction between the banks, which are never perfectly smooth, and the current, makes the point where the tail of a pool meets the bank a comfortable place for a trout to live. The rougher the bank, such as cobbles set into the edge, the more trout you'll find there. Often, too, the current will dig a deep slot near the bank, which forms a trench that is deeper than the water in the middle of the river.

Bends

So far we've looked at a stylized, symmetrical pool, where the main thread of current goes right down the middle. But these are rare. In looking for examples to examine and photograph when researching this book, I had a devil of a time finding a perfectly symmetrical pool. In most pools, the main current favors one side or the other. How does this change where trout will be?

A typical example is a bend pool. The current at the head of the pool flows toward one bank, forming a semicircular pool with a deep, fast side and a shallower, slower side. The force of the current, plus centrifugal force, digs a deep slot close to the bank. Because this outside of the bend is the deepest part of the pool, the part that gets the fastest flow and the most food, and is closest to cover, it will hold the most and best trout. Right? Not always.

In order to create a bend, water often flows against an unerodable surface, at an angle that can be from very oblique to 90 degrees. Whether there will be a lot of trout, or even any trout at all, on the outside of this bend depends on a couple of things: current speed and the smoothness of the outside bank. Water flowing along the outside bank combines the force of most of the river's current with centrifugal force, and unless there is a place for the trout to get out of the current, this apparent hot spot can be barren.

Undercut banks are said to be a prime spot to find trout, especially big ones. The current cuts under a stable grassy or rocky bank, forming an

Casting to the inside seam of a bend pool.

In this bend pool, where the current pushes against the far bank, it may be too fast for a trout at A; you'd more likely find a trout next to the bank at B.

area that never sees the direct light of day. These places have often disappointed me, especially at their upper ends. One in particular had always beckoned to me and never produced, so I put on a mask and went underwater. The head of this bend was undercut, but what I saw was an area that had been swept clean by the current—no rocks, logs, or anything to protect a trout from the current.

The outside of a bend *will* produce trout, however, if it is not smooth. Even a small projection from the bank, a jumble of boulders, or fallen trees—all will hold trout out of the force of the current. These places often harbor large trout; but it is difficult to get a natural drift here, making it tough to fool them. The trout are lying in slow water, yet just a few inches away is water that might be running at four or five feet per second. Your line drags the fly immediately, regardless of your angle of approach. My best luck on these fish has been from about 45 degrees upstream, throwing a lot of slack into the line.

Besides a rough bank, another factor will move trout into the outside of the bend—reduced flow. Goddard and Clarke remark that a trout will always be found within two to three yards of the outside of a bend, but look at the water they wrote about: chalkstreams. Because chalkstreams or spring creeks flow slowly in relation to freestone rivers, even at the outside of the bend I doubt if the current flows faster than that optimum 1.5 feet per second. They'll get more food on the outside of a bend without having to exhaust themselves in the process.

How do you tell if trout will favor the inside or the outside of a bend? If the outside of a bend strikes a bedrock bank hard enough to push water up onto the sides of the bank, that tells you the current on the outside may be too strong unless there is something to break the current. If the outside of the bend strikes a bank of gently sloping gravel, you know that the force of the current can't be too strong—otherwise it would flood right over the bank. In this kind of bend, I'd expect to find trout scattered throughout the bend, from one bank to another, maybe slightly favoring the outside.

In the slower flows of midsummer, even in the fast kind of bend, trout are likely to move into the outside from the lower part of a bend, or from the seam on the inside of the bend, when these two places become too shallow and barren of food. (More about these seasonal changes in a later chapter.)

On a typical bend pool, especially in the early to midseason, more trout will be found where the angle of the bend starts to diminish, and in the seam opposite the bend, than in the deep, fast part.

Where the current strikes the bank at close to a right angle, there will be three seams formed. First and probably the most productive one will be the seam opposite the elbow where the current strikes the bank. This seam often forms what fishermen call a shelving riffle, which is a riffle that gradually deepens into the pool. A shelving riffle shows up as a patch of lighter-colored bottom opposite the outside of the bend and will usually be gently riffled as opposed to the faster current—betrayed by white water and standing waves—of the center of the river and the outside of the bend. It's a productive spot that will often hold more than a couple of trout. They line up along the shelf and will be especially abundant where

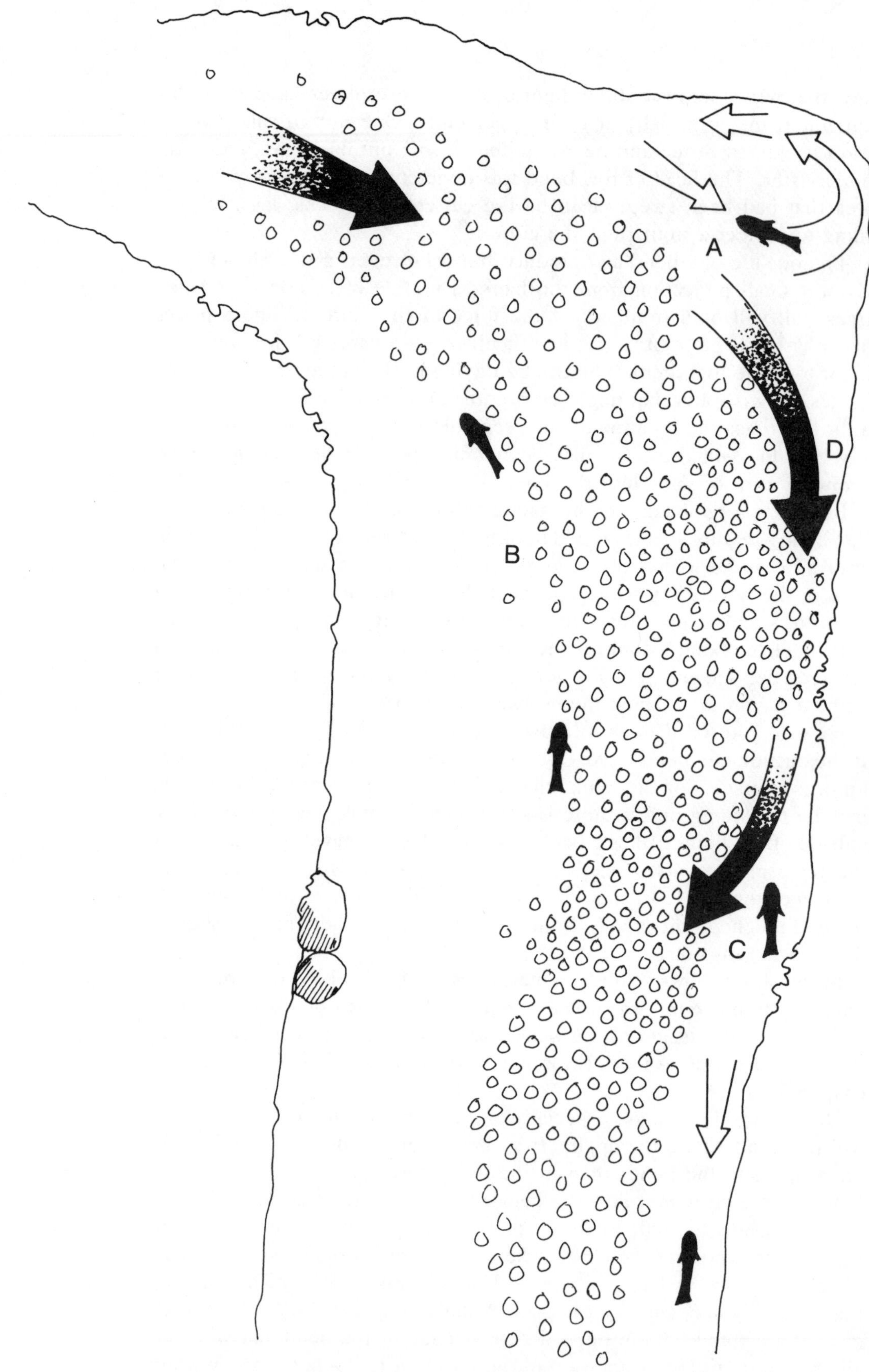

The three seams that may be formed when a fast current makes a sharp turn. A is a whirlpool current just upstream of the spot where the main current hits the bank. This seam may not always be present. B is the inside seam, and is always present, sometimes as a whirlpool. C is a seam formed where the current slows down and begins to pull toward the other bank. At D the bank is often undercut and is the place most fishermen pay the most attention to—but the current there may be too swift.

the depth changes from one to two feet deep. This is where the color starts to change, and you'll find this hot spot where the riffle starts to deepen as you go in a downstream direction and also on the edge of the shelf that touches the main current in the center of the river.

The second most productive seam will be right next to the bank, downstream of the elbow, where centrifugal force begins to push the main current back toward the center of the river. On the outside of this seam, between the seam and the bank, will be a smooth place on the surface. If the bank has other features that make it a good spot for a trout to live and feed, such as a jumble of rocks or a patch of alders, so much the better. Give it your complete attention.

Another seam will form just upstream of the place where the elbow of the current touches the bank. If the current is forced around at a sharp angle—nearing 90 degrees—this particular seam will be small and probably filled with silt, so it may not be worth fishing. If the angle of a bend is more oblique, the seam formed above the elbow will get longer and will provide more living space for a couple of nice trout. Alternatively, the elbow of the bend can get eroded, making a bend that kisses the bank, then angles away from the bank in a straight line until it touches the bank again, cutting off a little bay. In this bay is a whirlpool that defies the best

A slow bend pool. A good spot is the inside seam at A, but the current isn't too fast even at the outside of the bend at B—or even in the middle at C.

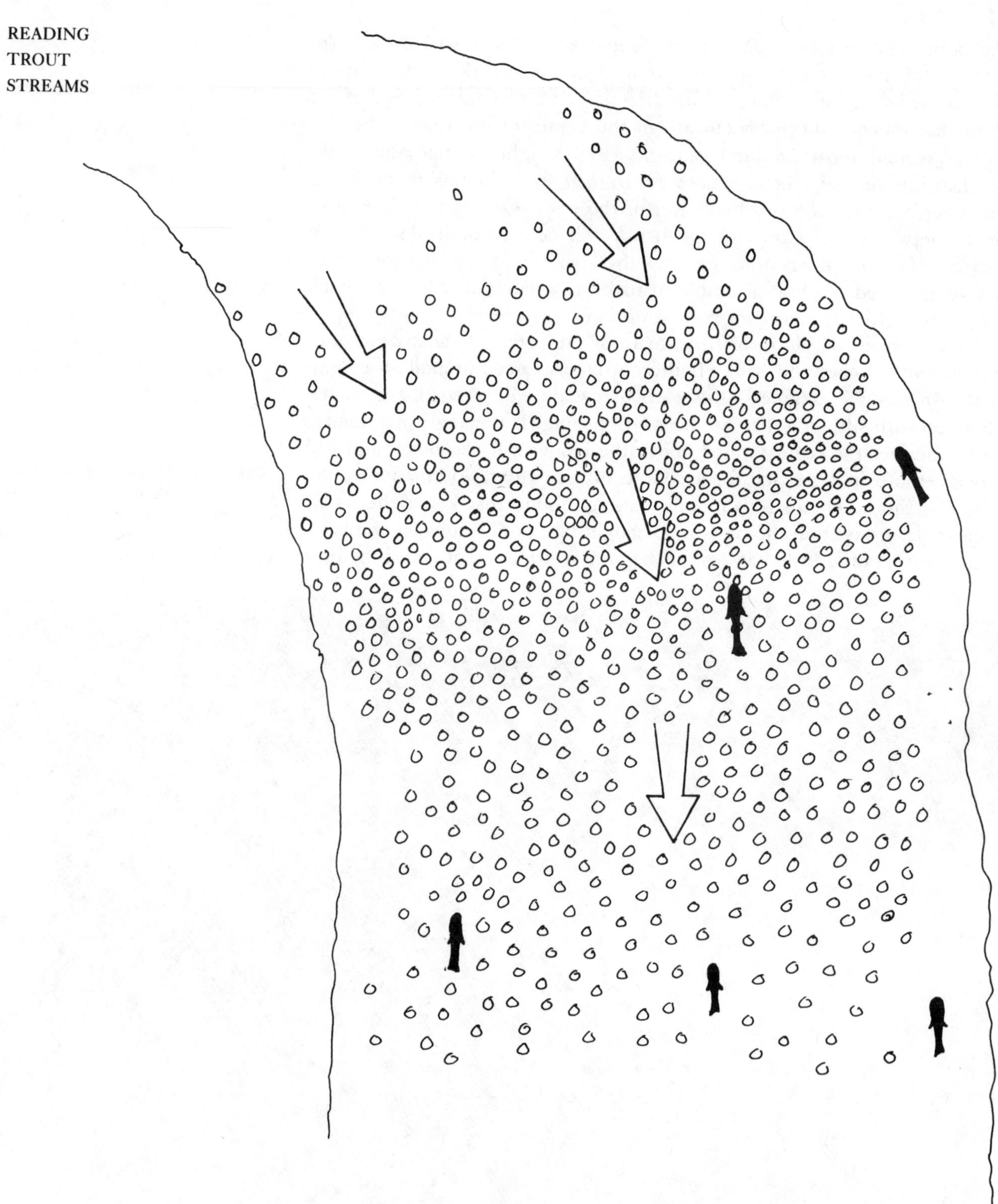

Possible lies in a slow bend pool. The trout are scattered throughout, especially where the riffle starts to flatten.

efforts of man and modern technology to get a drag-free drift. The trout invariably lie in the current against the far bank, facing downstream. The only problem is that to cast to them you have to put your line and leader over three or four currents of different speeds and directions if you use the typical across-stream presentation.

I caught my first cutthroat trout in a whirling seam like this. A friend of mine was running a ranch along the Snake River in Wyoming, and there were some spring creek tributaries to the Snake that ran through his property. We hacked through the brush to fish a side channel that he assured me hadn't been fished all season, and in the seam above a sharp bend were three or four cutthroats sipping blue-winged olives with the confidence of an elephant stuffing peanuts into his mouth. Cutthroats are supposed to be on the Neanderthal side of the trout family, so I was ready to take all of them in a half-dozen casts. It took me about two hours longer than I thought to hook even two of them, but I came away from that seam with a new respect for what a couple feet of conflicting currents can do for the "intelligence" of cutthroats.

In bend pools, the main current usually continues down the bank on the same side as the bend. Look for the bubble line that indicates where all the food is drifting. Look for silt or debris on the bottom that indicates where the food isn't drifting. Often the barren side of a one-sided pool will be obviously too shallow to hold trout, but it can also be just as deep as the "good" side and might fool you. If there is three feet of water on the side opposite the main current with little flow, yet two feet of water on the side where the current is running, your trout are more likely to be in the shallow side.

There is a slow quarter-mile-long pool on the Delaware that consistently produces large brown trout for me. Halfway down this huge pool, in flat, featureless water, is a spot no more than six feet square where they're often rising when the rest of the pool is quiet. I found this place by carefully watching for rises, not by reading the stream.

Last year, I finally realized what intelligent reading of the water could have told me years ago. The riffle at the head of the pool comes in at a slight angle, and if you draw an imaginary line through the pool, the current from that riffle intersects the bank at my hot spot. The pool is too slow to show any obvious current patterns, but by imagining its course like you'd estimate a billiard shot you could discover my secret, too.

Split Pools

Some of the pools you fish might split at the head because of a boulder or a piece of bedrock that divides the current. Great! One side might form a bend pool, the other may run straight down the center of the pool. Instead of having two seams at the head of the pool, you have four, so this pool has double the number of prime spots at the head as one that is symmetrical. Follow the current threads of both pieces down through the pool, through the middle, right to the tail, and you'll be plotting the areas where your casts will be most productive.

A pool with split currents. The best spot in this photo would be where the currents converge.

Sometimes the seams from the two currents will stay separated throughout the pool, especially when there is a large obstruction at the head of a pool. But often the two currents will converge. When this happens, they are never flowing at exactly the same speed or direction, so some turbulence and a dead spot are formed. These places are often overlooked, because there is no solid object to slow down the current. A trout that is lying in the dead spot between these two seams has not one but two main currents bringing him food, so he can dart to either side when he spots a choice morsel drifting by. The apex of the "Y" where two currents meet is an especially productive area.

Waterfall Pools

Waterfall pools are appealing to the eyes and ears, and they present some special problems when trying to figure out where the trout are. I caught my first trout in a big waterfall pool in a state park in New York

In this waterfall pool, I would look for trout anywhere you don't see foam—especially in front of the rocks at the lower right corner of the photo.

State, and I'll bet if your first trout wasn't caught below a waterfall, at least it was the first kind of pool that you thought might hold trout. Where trout are below a waterfall depends on the amount of vertical drop in the falls. The greater the drop, the more energy is expended on the bottom underneath the falls, and the less likely trout are to be found in the foaming white water.

I once had the enviable job of fishing for a video production. One of the scenes called for a trout to be caught and released in a pretty spot, and I was dead-set against faking it with hatchery trout or on a private stocked stream. We found a spot on a small stream that looked like the cover of a *Vermont Life* magazine. Once the camera got rolling, I fired a confident cast to the base of a waterfall, right at the edge of the foaming water. More casts followed, and the expensive tape kept rolling without a subject. All of the current in the pool converged in a shallow spot in the tail, at the edge of a ledge rock that extended to form an underwater shelf. There was a soft rise in the shallow water. On my first cast, a fish twice the size I expected grabbed the dry fly, thumped a couple of times, and broke off.

Watching the tape later, I heard myself whisper "Wow," and then a second later, "Did you see how big that fish was?" I had a wireless mike

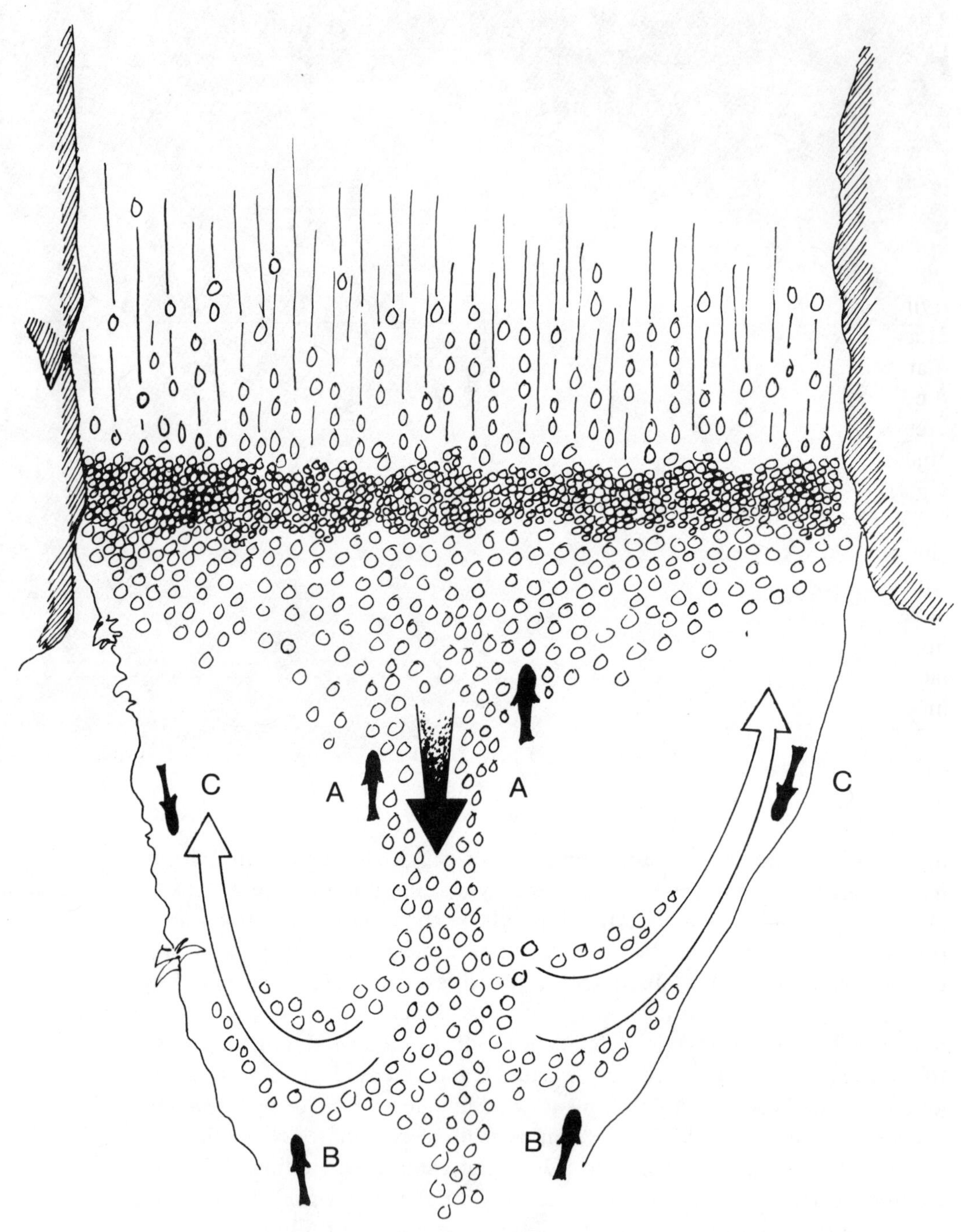

Lies in a waterfall pool. The fish at A are at the edge of the white water. The trout at B are in the tail of the pool. Waterfall pools are usually short in relation to their width and have whirlpools, so the trout at C are facing downstream.

on and the script didn't call for any dialogue, but the cameraman missed the action anyway. Although I never got to see how large the trout was, I did get to examine the pool in detail, because the cameraman had been shooting from a vantage point high above the water, so every detail of the pool was visible. Yes, there was a nice deep hole below the falls but there wasn't any place for a trout to feed comfortably as there were no big rocks to break the current. At the tail of the pool, where the current converged in a single spot, there was a smooth, predictable flow that brought every piece of drifting food through a single slot three feet wide.

The same amount of food was drifting through the base of the waterfall but to intercept a mayfly nymph or an ant struggling on the surface, a trout would have to struggle through turbulence worse than a Piper Cub trying to climb through a hurricane. But doesn't the deep pool at the base of a waterfall offer a trout superb protection? Yes. A trout underneath all that foam is almost invincible. But I'm not so sure that the fish we see at the base of waterfalls when swimming haven't been spooked there by our presence, because most fishermen I talk to don't catch many there. The object of fly fishing, or any kind of fishing, is to find trout that are feeding, not trout that are hiding out.

Waterfall pools are usually short in relation to their width, and they almost always have eddies or whirlpools on either side that extend the whole length of the pool. Thus, it's possible that a trout lying in the tail of the pool five feet from the bank is facing upstream as you try to sneak up on him from downstream, and another fish two feet from the bank is facing *you*. Watch those currents carefully or all the fish in the pool *will* be hiding under the waterfall.

Waterfalls are natural congregation points for migrating fish, either because those migrating upstream are resting before trying to jump the falls, or because trout that washed over the falls in a downstream migration earlier are trying to get back up. Although this book is about nonmigratory stream trout as opposed to salmon and steelhead, even nonmigratory trout move under certain conditions that we'll explore in a later chapter. I don't know how high a falls has to be before it is impassable to trout but I would imagine that any straight vertical drop of over six feet would be impassable to a foot-long fish.

So a waterfall pool that looks impassable to trout might hold more trout than you would think just by looking at the banks and by the number of bottom obstructions. The pool just above a high waterfall may hold fewer trout than you'd expect, because floods or predators may push fish over the falls.

Junction Pools

When a tributary enters a river, or where two rivers converge, a junction pool is formed. Let's say we have a small stream entering a larger river. Two seams will be formed—one adjacent to the flow of the river, the other between the bank and the flow of the trib, which has now

The seam formed at the junction of two rivers is a fine place for trout. Besides the attraction of currents of two different speeds meeting, one river might offer a different insect hatch or a more favorable temperature.

become part of the river. Both of these seams can be productive, but one may be better than the other. For instance, the flow in the main river might be fast, so trout might prefer the inside seam, closest to the bank. Maybe there's a hatch of big, juicy mayflies in the main river. In this case you might find more trout in the outside seam, adjacent to the main flow of the river where the food is coming from. But the most important case, and the factor that makes tribs so important, is when the water temperature of the trib is different from that in the main river. (This will be covered in a later chapter on the daily and seasonal changes in a trout stream.)

5
Riffles, Flats, and Pocket Water

A run is the area water takes from one elevation to a lower one. In a pool, the slope of the bottom is fairly flat, so the water settles into a basin and has a chance to form a distinct head, tail, and middle. Between pools, or when the slope of the land drops for an extended distance, water flows through a channel that might be shallow and carpeted with fine gravel (a riffle), through a relatively deep, narrow channel with a quick change in slope (a chute), through a flat piece of land like a meadow where the slope of the land changes gradually (flats), or through either type of channel with the bottom covered with boulders (pocket water). In every kind of run except a flat, a trout needs more protection than he would in an adjacent pool because the current is swifter.

Some runs lose elevation so fast that there is no place for a trout to live. The swift water flows over a bottom so smooth, having been washed clean by the current, that there is no visible turbulence. These are often called chutes by fishermen and you can see why. There is a chute like this on the Willowemoc that has one lonely boulder in the middle of the run. I can always count on taking one or two fish from behind this boulder on a Leadwing Coachman wet fly; that fly isn't better than any others but I first took a trout there ten years ago and I have never felt a need to try any other fly. I've also never caught or seen a fish feeding in any other place in this run.

The chute in the center of the photo offers a fast current with a smooth gravel bottom—not a desireable place for a trout to live.

Most runs, however, are not as impetuous in their journey to the sea, and are as good a place to catch trout as a classic pool. In fact, a typical run in most trout streams would be of moderate depth and speed—about the same as the middle of a pool on the same river. It just won't have a distinct head and tail, and might run a little faster. I suggest that you fish most runs exactly as you would a pool. The Battenkill and the AuSable in Michigan have few classic pools. Most of the areas we call pools on these rivers are really runs, but we call them pools and nobody seems to suffer. Let's examine the special kinds of runs that present different challenges: riffles, flats, and pocket water.

A riffle is any run that is so shallow that turbulence from the bottom is mirrored in the surface of the water throughout the run, resulting in an almost continuous pockmarking of the surface. The depth can be anywhere from an inch to three feet. Any deeper than three feet and the turbulence from the bottom won't get to the surface so the water will look smooth. Then you have a typical run. Riffles are a special case because of their shallowness.

Some fishermen might call this place on the King's River a run. It has a head, middle, and tail, and can be looked at as a pool with a fast current.

Flats are often long and seemingly monotonous pieces of water. They flow through flat stretches of land. The most typical flat that you might encounter in the West would be one of those high-altitude meadow streams that meanders between grassy bends. In the East, such waters are commonly associated with boggy brook trout streams, the kind that run for miles through alders and black spruce with scarcely a riffle.

Pocket water is a deep riffle or run that is studded with boulders, anywhere from bowling ball to elephant-sized. Most often the turbulence from one rock intersects the turbulence of others. If you just throw a couple of big rocks into a run you have a run with a couple of big rocks in it—but not pocket water. A riffle can run into pocket water, or a river can have pocket water on one side and a typical run on the other.

Riffles

Most riffles are considered too shallow and too fast to hold decent trout. They are the insect producers in a stream, where the water is shallow enough to let the sun reach the bottom so algae can thrive and bugs

In a shallow riffle, the place where the water looks dark and slick, and you can't make out the stones on the bottom, may be the only place to hold trout. There is a deep pocket in the right center of the photo.

can feed. Riffles are the place where young-of-the-year trout, which range from less than an inch long to six inches, can live without much worry of being preyed upon by their parents. True. But riffles can hold trout, not just for short feeding sprees, but for a whole season if conditions are right.

What do you look for? If the riffle is mostly less than a foot deep I'd look for deeper spots. How do you find them? Look for changes in color, where the water darkens. If the water is clear, look for places where you can't make out the stones on the bottom. But there is a way of finding these deeper pockets, even in late evening when you can't make out any details other than the surface of the water—slicks.

Experienced fishermen search out slicks without knowing what they're looking for. While I was researching this book, I kept asking myself how I *knew* there was a pocket in a particular place. It took hours of staring at the water and at photographs of water to figure out why slicks betray deeper water. In a riffle, the water is so shallow that the roughness of the bottom is betrayed by the surface. If the surface of the water in one place is smooth, you know that the bottom has suddenly become as smooth as glass (unlikely), or that the water is moving slower, or that the water here is so deep that the turbulence isn't getting to the surface. Either slower or deeper water will be a location that may hold trout. Maybe this is common sense to *you,* but it wasn't to me, and I had never seen this explanation in print before.

You have two ways of finding the deeper pockets in riffles—though even finding a pocket doesn't guarantee a hotbed of trout. In a river with wide graveled banks, I'd look out toward the center of the river, or at least twenty feet from shore, where a trout has enough room to run to the depths when a streamside predator approaches. In a stream with heavily wooded banks, sometimes the best spot in a riffle is right up along the bank. The water is usually a little deeper here, and streamside brush and logs provide some protection.

If the pocket in a riffle is out in the open, not near any other piece of deep water or a big rock or log, make sure it's big and deep enough to hide the trout if he starts feeling insecure.

Most fishermen use riffles as avenues to get from one place to another, because we don't disturb any "good" water, and riffles are the easiest

This riffle at the head of a run always produces trout for me in the early season but probably not in the areas you'd think. At A there is a swirly slick that is too unpredictable for the fish to hold in. The central channel, B, is also too fast (note the standing waves). The slick at C offers a gentle but steady current and just enough depth. I've seen as many as twenty trout rising in the little slick.

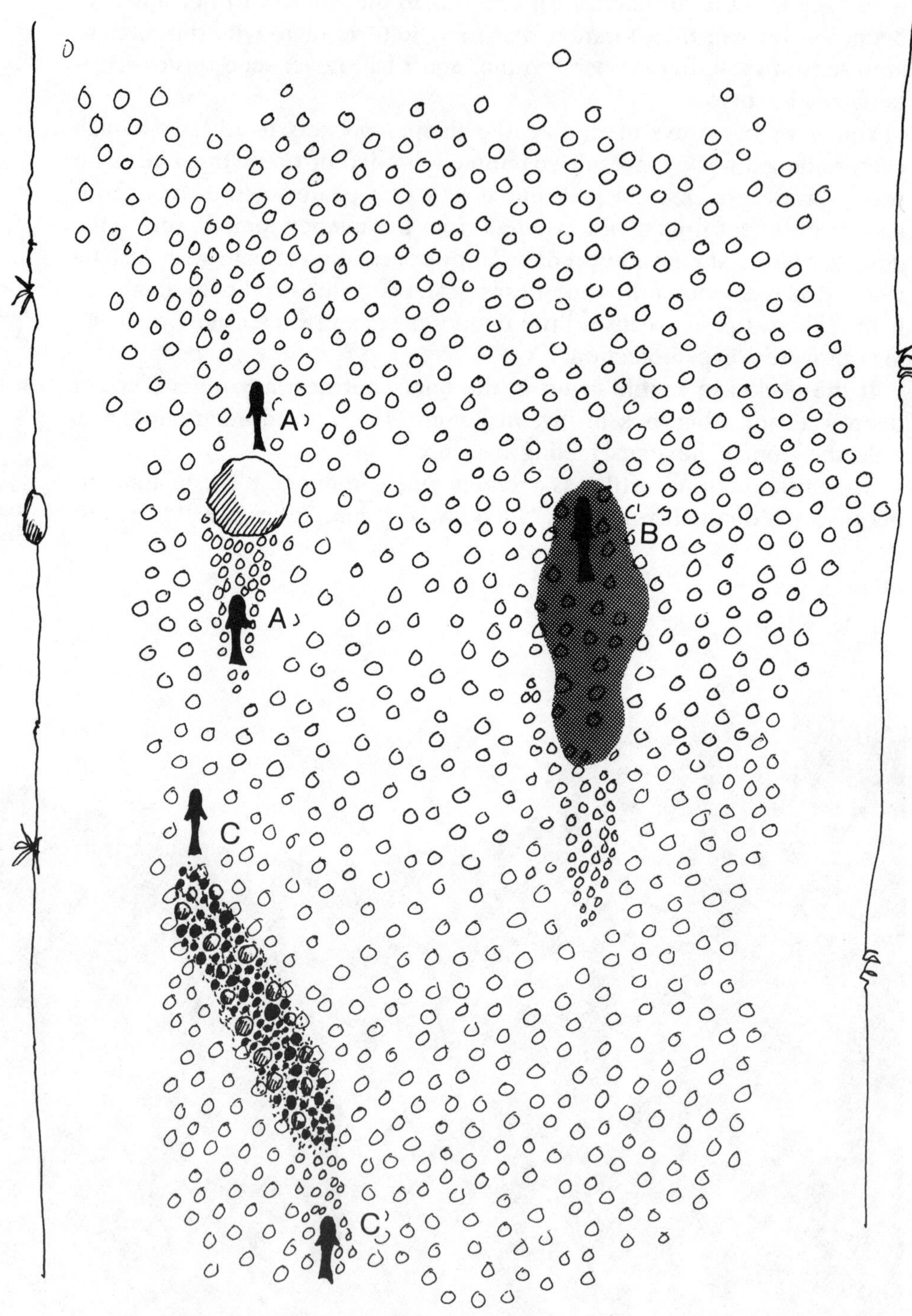

Places to look for trout in a shallow riffle: A, in front of and behind rocks that dig small depressions in the river bed and break the current; B, in deeper slots that show up as slicks on the surface; and C, in front of and behind gravel bars.

places in a river to cross. There is one riffle in the Battenkill that I usually blundered across to get to the good side of a favorite pool. One afternoon in May, during a heavy Hendrickson spinner fall, I spotted a nose poking out of one of those slicks I mentioned above. Good trout in shallow riffles aren't common, but when you find them they're easy—no drag problems because the current flows at a uniform speed, a riffle on the surface to hide you and your casting mistakes, not much time to inspect your fly because the current is fast. He took on the second or third cast and really made a fuss in the shallow water.

The funny thing is, I've never seen a trout of any size in that spot again. And you can bet I've looked. But floods can move these pockets in riffles around a lot each season because the bottom in a riffle is composed of little stones that don't stay put for long. Something happened to the bottom in this little pocket that made it less desirable to trout.

If the riffle is deeper than two feet throughout, reading a stream can be tough because *all* of the water looks good. This is the situation on the Delaware, where the riffles can extend for hundreds of feet across and downstream. Every time I fish a new riffle on that river, I feel helpless and stupid, unless I'm fishing with someone who has fished it before. The logical place to start looking is where the riffle starts to flatten out and lose all those little bumps on the surface of the water. Here the trout can rest and wait for the hordes of insects being washed down from the riffle, but they don't have to fight the current to feed.

Look for other places to narrow down the search. You can't blind-fish that whole giant riffle! Larger rocks, bigger than the rubble on the bottom, will show up as Vs in the water. You already know how to fish these—look for the dead spots and the focal point. Gravel bars will often form in these big riffles, and they'll usually angle downstream. You'll be able to spot bars by the slick on the upstream side and by a seam that trails downstream of the end of the bar. The best spots in relation to a bar like this are the crotch at the upper end of the upstream side of the bar and in the seam that trails just below the downstream end.

FLATS

In flats, like riffles, you may not find trout everywhere. They are often limited by the amount of food-producing riffles and by the rocks that provide shelter from predators. Any time you have a paucity of rocks, look to the banks. Especially in flats. Review the section on banks in Chapter 3 to refresh yourself on the kinds that attract trout.

The few riffles that you find in this kind of water have concentrations of trout, although they may not be where you think they are. Though riffles produce great quantities of food, trout in long, slow flats will position themselves downstream some distance from a riffle in a flat, probably because in a flat they don't need to be right up in the faster current to take advantage of its food-producing qualities. I've had my best luck in the spot where the riffle stops "riffling." Here trout can feed on drifting insects without fighting the current. Don't ever forget that trout are lazy and efficient feeders.

There's a nice riffle at the head of a 200-foot flat on the Battenkill, in a spot that I once spent almost every evening of a season fishing. The riffle seems attractive to trout—it's two to three feet deep, has a nice undercut bank on one side, and is overhung with willows. Yet I never saw a trout feed there, nor did I ever catch one fishing blind. Where the riffle flattened was the place where the trout started and they continued down through the flat, distributed around any log or bush that hung over the bank. Later that summer, I fished a huge tailwater river that flows through desert country in Wyoming. This river, the name and location of which I had to swear to secrecy, consisted of big riffles that spread out into flats that were 100 yards long and half a mile wide. Nothing like my lush, intimate little Battenkill. But I wasn't smart enough to learn the lesson of that summer and apply it to this river. It took a full morning of unproductive casting in the riffles before I wised up and fished the less interesting but spectacularly more productive flats below.

In rivers with extensive flats like the Battenkill, concentrate your efforts well below riffles, on the outside of bends, and in areas with good bank cover, as this fisherman is doing.

When flats meander through meadows, the bends act as the heads and tails of pools. At the "head" will usually be an undercut bank, and in the case of slow meadow runs like this, the outside of the bend, where the undercut forms, will not be too fast for trout—in fact, unlike a typical

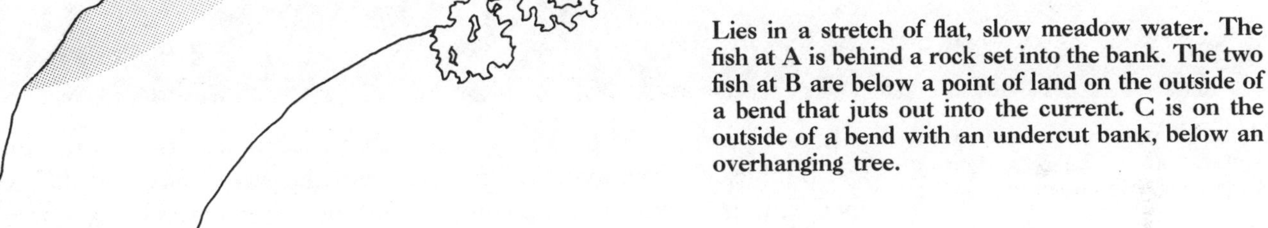

Lies in a stretch of flat, slow meadow water. The fish at A is behind a rock set into the bank. The two fish at B are below a point of land on the outside of a bend that juts out into the current. C is on the outside of a bend with an undercut bank, below an overhanging tree.

bend, the inside seam may not provide enough food for a fish because the current won't bring it to him fast enough. Below the bend on the outside bank is the place to concentrate your efforts.

Pocket Water

People who have never fished for trout look at pocket water and exclaim, "A fish could never live in that!" But trout thrive in such foamy, swirling water. The neat thing about pocket water, from a fly fisherman's point of view, is that the trout living there will invariably be insect feeders and will readily take flies. Night-feeding cannibals that cruise looking for minnows and crayfish will park themselves somewhere else. It's too hard to move around in pocket water for that kind of feeding behavior.

A beckoning piece of pocket water, with all the water types a fisherman will encounter.

Look at a piece of pocket water, paying special attention to the foam and bubbles. Notice that, unlike in a riffle, the water moves at different speeds, from very fast in the lanes that are not interrupted by boulders to completely calm behind the rocks. In fact, one of the best ways to read pocket water is to follow the bubble line through the run. It will tell you where the food is going, but it will also tell you where the current is moderate enough to hold a trout without exhausting him. The prime places in a piece of pocket water will be the areas where the slower spots butt against the food lanes.

Another way to fish pocket water is to do it by water type. Because pocket water is composed of fast and slow currents and big rocks, you'll find every kind of surface wrinkle that appears in rivers—standing waves, white water, slicks with a smooth surface, slicks with a swirly surface, and gentle riffles. This is the way I fish pocket water if I'm in a hurry to get to the pool above, or if I'm in a large river and have no idea where the fish are.

The first thing you do is eliminate standing waves and white water. Standing waves indicate rough turbulence underneath, too much for a trout to tolerate. White water seldom holds trout because it knocks them around too much, but also because they can't see what's going on—they can't see their food and they can't spot predators. Not that you don't want to toss your fly in this kind of water. You can use these areas to get a

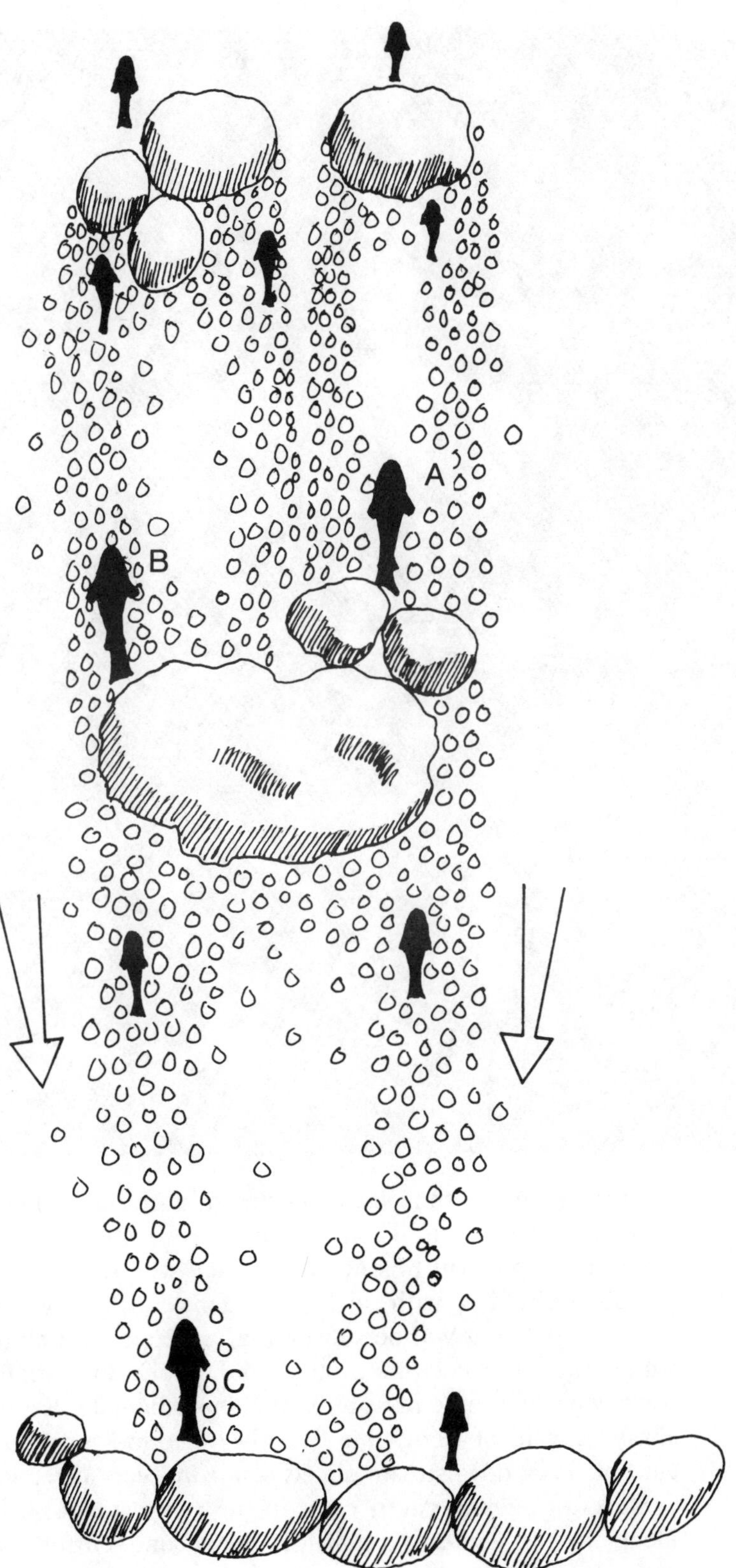

Possible lies in a piece of pocket water. The largest trout will be found at A, B, and C, where the focal point of one rock intersects the cushion of another.

A closer look at some pocket water. I would eliminate the white water at A and the standing waves at B as probable trout lies. The swirly slicks at C are possibilities but I would place my fly in the smooth slicks, D, and in the gentle riffles at E.

good drift toward the places on the side of and below white water and standing waves. But when you plan your strategy, just bear in mind where the trout will be and where they won't.

Now we're left with slicks and gentle riffles, which are the places where the current will be slower and/or deeper. I'd eliminate those slicks where the surface swirls around like smoke in a drafty room, because trout don't like to be in water that's unpredictable. Swirly currents are not always devoid of trout, but I've always found more in slicks where the current flows downstream slowly—not in every direction at once.

Slicks in pocket water, even in the swiftest rivers, seem to offer that ideal one- to one-and-a-half-feet-per-second current speed. Despite a rough bottom, the turbulence you see on the surface is minimal when the water is deep enough so that the turbulence is all but spent when it reaches the surface, or where the current is so slow that little turbulence forms, or both. Those that are too shallow you can eliminate by checking to see if the color of the water there is much lighter than water in sur-

Notice how the rocks at the head and tail define this mini-pool in a stretch of pocket water, and how the slope of the water seems to plateau.

rounding areas. Seldom will you have to worry about places where the current is *too* slow, unless the water level is at extreme late-summer levels, and then the current will be stagnant only behind the larger rocks.

I once found a deep slot in a brawling stretch of the upper Connecticut River by spotting one of these slicks in the center of the run. It was a place where I had never seen a trout rising, though I had fished the run for three years in a row. It was a slow day and I decided to try a big black stonefly nymph with split shot and an indicator, western style, as the water in this part of the river looks more like Montana than Vermont. It worked, and since that day I've always been able to pull two or three fourteen-inch rainbows out of that slick—but only if I get a completely dead drift right in the slot, which is only about three feet wide. A foot too far to the right or left yields nothing.

Your eye should also be drawn to gentle riffles when you look over a piece of pocket water. Such water is moving at a steady pace but not so fast that it forms standing waves or white water. It has everything a trout needs—predictable currents, a steady food supply, and shelter from the fastest currents. This water differs from a slick in that it may be moving faster than the water in the slick, or it may be shallow enough to reflect the roughness of the bottom in surface turbulence. It's a little tough to describe the kind of riffle I'm talking about. If you pull the hairs on your arm gently and look at the skin underneath, this is the texture you're looking for.

There is one more way of telling where the trout will be. Often a bunch of rocks will line up in the current, forming what looks like the head of a pool on a smaller scale. Then, downstream a ways, there will be another pile of rocks that backs the water up, forming the tail of a mini-pool. In between these two piles of rocks will be a nice slick, due to the slowing down of the current from the rocks above and the deepening and slowing action of the lower pile of rocks. If you step back from the river and look at one of these spots and look at its slope in relation to the rest of the run, you'll see that the river doesn't appear to drop at so rapid a rate, forming a "plateau" in the descent of the pocket water.

Fish this miniature pool just like you would any other pool. The best place in one of these pockets is usually the tail end, where the fish back up against the pile of rocks, enjoying the view and the food and the protection from the nasty current beyond their haven. Just below where the white water at the head of the pocket ends is also a prime spot, as are the seams on either side.

6
Big Rivers and Little Brooks

Most of the trout streams you will fish will be somewhere between ten feet and 100 yards wide. People seem to have trouble reading the water in streams at either extreme but they're no different from "typical" trout streams when you realize the special constraints placed upon the trout that live in them.

The most important part of evaluating brooks that are barely as wide as your rod is long or rivers that an NFL kicker would have trouble booting a ball across is to step back and look at the water with all 180° of your vision. You hear such clichés as "fish a gigantic river as you would a little brook, dividing it up in your mind before you start." Horse manure. Turn an experienced fisherman loose on an unfamiliar river the size of the Missouri and watch how he handles the situation. First he'll find a place where he can get a panoramic view of as much of the river as possible, preferably a high bank. Then he might walk three-quarters of a mile to the spot he's selected. Next, he will get into position to fish either the bank or the center of the river. Only after all this jockeying for position will he divide the river up into smaller pieces.

If you follow a small stream connoisseur around for a day, you'll see he goes through similar rituals. After a look at the lay of the land (literally, because slope plays an important part in reading small streams), he will poke his flies into one pool, take a glance upstream, pass up thirty or forty feet of runs or small pools, and make a beeline for a place that seems to transfix him like a batter concentrating on an incoming pitch.

Small Brooks

A couple of years ago I guided a friend from California, a master at fishing the awesome steelhead rivers in the northern part of his state, on a miniature Vermont headwater stream. The most vivid memory I have of the evening was his delight at a dusky field sparkling with fireflies. Although they don't have fireflies in California, there are plenty of tiny streams but Mack had never bothered with them. It showed. His casting and streamcraft were superb, but he put his fly in all the wrong places, spooking more trout than he rose.

I could afford to be smug. I had learned small-stream fishing from a master, the late Tony Skilton, who died from lymphoma at the age of thirty-nine. How I wish he had told me more about what he looked for in a small stream! We talked a lot about tackle and technique, how a big dry fly on a 3X tippet was more effective than dinky flies on light leaders, things he had learned on the mountain streams of northern Pennsylvania and brought to Vermont. But I can only remember discussing stream reading once. We were exploring a cascading mountain brook and I wondered out loud why a particular stretch wasn't producing. We had both been teaching in a shooting school at the time and Tony mumbled something about "too much drop at the heel and comb." These are measurements on a shotgun that determine the slope of the stock from the end of the barrels to the end of the stock. "What?" I asked. "Look at the way the land slopes so steeply," he said. "There's no place where the stream levels off enough for the trout to have a comfortable place to live."

Indeed, you can fish a mountain brook that spills from one icy bathtub to another by inspecting the slope of the surface of the water. Look what happens: wherever the flow of the brook is slowed enough to form a pool that will hold a couple of trout, the water will not slant as much in a downstream direction as it will when plunging down a steep incline. A boulder that takes up the whole stream channel can do it, as can a slight plateau in the land through which the stream flows. In a small brook you'll find few backwaters or refuges from the current in a run that connects two pools because the main flow invariably stretches from one bank to the other.

In previous chapters I belittled the importance of depth and cover to trout. Now I'm telling you they are essential—at least in small streams. Terrestrial mammals seldom threaten trout in rivers, but if a trout lives in a brook that is two arm-lengths of a raccoon wide, he'd better have some protection. Raccoons and mink prowl the banks of most trout streams looking for carrion, frogs, and crayfish, but they relish trout if one is dumb enough to lie unprotected near shore.

Because the banks hold more danger to trout, nice-looking pockets along the side of a brook may not be as full of fish as they seem at first glance. The smaller the brook, the more likely the fish will be found in the center of the river in the deepest water.

Will all trout be found out in the center of small brooks? Not always. If the bank offers a steep boulder that would make a precarious perch for a predator, or if a log that has fallen along the bank is wide enough to

The right-hand bank in this tiny brook trout stream offers depth and protection without giving a predator an easy perch.

shelter a trout when danger threatens, a deep place along the bank may be a productive place to cast your Royal Wulff.

Depth is all-important in this kind of trout stream because here we're not looking at just any old small trout stream. You get into a special case when you have to check behind you before you make *every* cast, and you resign yourself to passing up a good percentage of the pools because nothing short of a worm threaded into a tangle of brush will pull a trout out of some of the pools.

Reading a brook involves finding the deepest water and then looking it over to make sure that a trout who lives there will not be eaten by the first mink to slink along. How deep is deep enough? Tony and I had a running contest to see how narrow a stream could be and one of us still take a trout from it; I believe he set the record at fifteen inches—the brook was fifteen inches wide; the trout was barely six. Still, as I remember, we never took even a small trout from a pool that was less than eight inches deep. Let's consider this the minimum depth in brooks, as I doubt you'll ever be masochistic enough to fish brooks as tiny as we did. And limiting yourself to water this deep or deeper will eliminate 90 percent of the water in small brooks.

The kind of brooks that plunge down the side of a mountain are the most common variety and are easy to read because the pools are obvious and the runs between the pools are so fast that you can eliminate half the water at once. You'll seldom find much of a meander in one, whether it is in the Appalachians or the Sierras or the Rockies.

Not so obvious is where to find the trout once you've found a likely pool. If the head and tail of the pool are as deep as the middle, you will invariably find the trout either tucked in at the tail, right up against the last rocks before it spills over, or in the seams at the head. Only if the head or the tail of the pool are less than eight inches deep and the middle is deeper will you find trout in the middle—or if the middle offers a great piece of cover like a big rock or sunken log. I know this is an unusually strong statement to make in a discipline that is governed by mother nature and her shopping bag full of variables, but I fish this kind of stream on my lunch hour all season long, and the trout rarely stray from these places. Besides, Joe Humphreys, author of the savvy book *Joe Humphreys's Trout Tactics* will tell you the exact same thing—and his brooks are hundreds of miles from mine.

Some brooks do not have well-defined pools. Instead, they are composed of stretches of miniature pocket water, with water bouncing from one rock to another in a frothy, random pattern. Where the water is less than a foot deep, it takes more than a single rock to make a haven for a trout. Just as you would in "big" pocket water, look for places where several rocks dam up the water to form miniature pools. Those pockets with a decent collection of rocks at both the head and the tail of the pocket will hold the most trout, as they slow the current down and provide the most depth.

Brooks do not offer as much food to trout as do rivers, even if you look at the food supply on a number-of-insects-per-square-foot basis. There are no vast shallow riffles, which act as the pastures of trout streams. What does this tell you when fishing a brook? First, it tells you that a pool the size of a coffee table will hold one, two, or maybe three trout. There is not enough food in a tiny pool to pack them in like kippers, and the trout will be more widely spaced than they may be in a river. Don't fool around with casts in places that look just okay. The fish will be found in the one or two juicy spots that beg for a size 14 Irresistible.

Second—watch the bubbles. Watch the debris. The fish will be right under their cafeteria line, not sitting in the janitor's closet. If the bubbles are skewed toward the right side of the tail of the pool, don't bother with the left—until you're satisfied that the trout on the right are either spooked or not eating.

Brooks that run through flatter land are much the same—the best places are the tails and the seams at the heads of the pools. But brooks that run through meadows and flatter woodland areas are different because they don't have the large rocks that mountain brooks offer for cover. Luckily they have meanders. Remember when talking about bends I put the most importance on the inside seam? In meadow brooks, the outside may be the best place to find a trout because it may be the only place in the pool that offers sufficient depth and safe cover.

Because the main current of a brook is not as swift as that of a river, the outside of the bend, ordinarily a spot that is too rigorous for a trout to hold comfortably, can be tolerated. The outsides of these bends are often

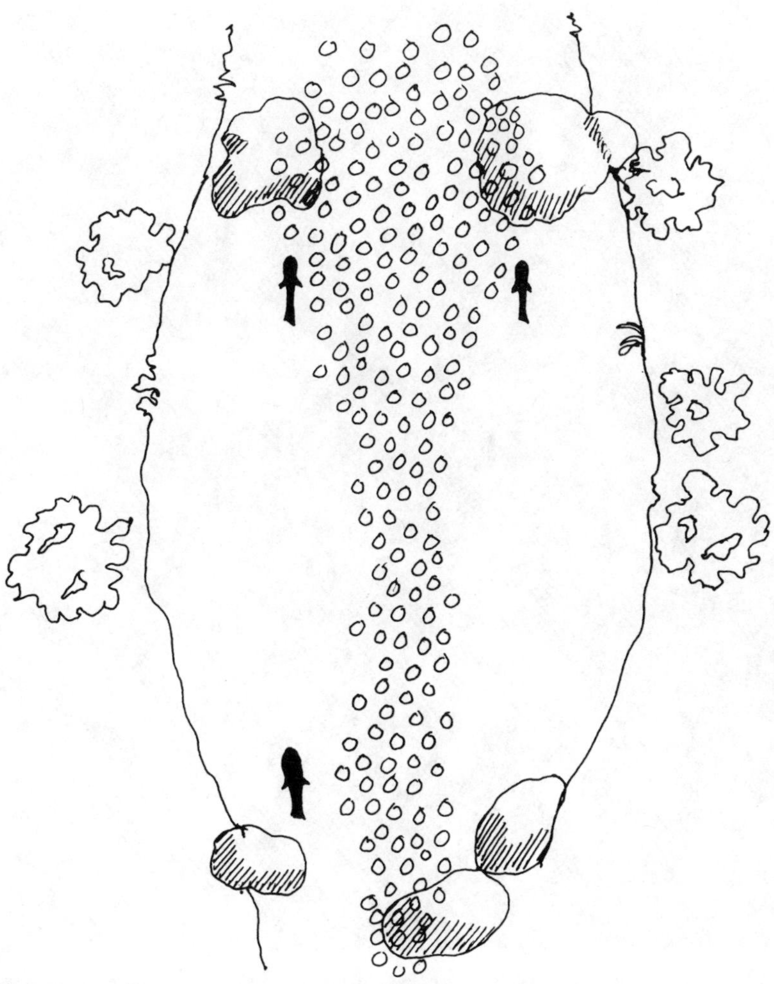

Lies in a pool or pocket of a small brook. Fish often occupy only the best spots at the head and tail.

undercut as well. An undercut bank in a large river is just one of many places to find trout—in a brook it may be the only place a trout can survive for long.

When I was growing up outside of Rochester, New York, I found a wild brook trout stream that ran down through the fourth hole of a suburban golf course. The best way to fish it was with a worm, but my early experiments with flies showed me that if I let a White Marabou streamer drift along an undercut bank, a brook trout with nearly every color of the spectrum would dart out to grab it—but only if the fly was within an inch of the edge of the undercut. Otherwise it would be ignored, or else I'd see a tentative flash under the edge of the bank. I never thought of this stream as having pools or runs. It was a series of undercuts, and I named each one, just like the pools on those faraway streams like the Beaverkill or the Yellowstone.

A pocket in a small stream formed by two small groups of rocks. This one always holds two eight-inch brook trout—one at the head and one at the tail.

A tiny stream with just a trickle running through it, but the undercut on the far bank, betrayed by the steep bank and overhanging trees, may hold a surprisingly large trout.

By the look of the bubble line in this Pennsylvania brook, I would expect trout in the tail to be on the left side.

From the air, it's easy to spot what should be the three best places in a meadow brook—the three outside bends at A, B, and C. I've spent much time fishing this water and our aerial observations are entirely correct.

Meadow brooks can suddenly swell into giant pools with the aid of beavers. You would think a beaver pond on a stream teeming with native brookies would hold some trophies, but did you know that beaver ponds can be sterile when it comes to trout life? Here is what happens: when beavers first dam a brook, it fills with fresh water and nutrients from the flooded land and, of course, trout. Suddenly not limited by the amount of food they could scrounge from the current, and being able to cruise lazily for their meals, the trout experience a growth spurt and get fatter than those in the surrounding brook. Unfortunately, as the years go by, the pond fills with silt, gets shallow, and the water becomes too warm for trout in the summertime. The cover that depth offered may disappear as well. The process can take three years or as many as ten, depending on the size of the pond and the flow of the current through it.

Trout are easy to find in a beaver pond. Because they cruise around, they can be anywhere, but the two best places are where the brook runs in, because of the food supply, and at the base of the dam, where the water is deepest.

Reading the water here is not as important as being able to tell the age of the pond at a glance. First, look at the trees in the flooded pond. Do they still have leaves, bark, and buds, or are they smooth and gray? Is the

The old and dead trees in this beaver pond tell you that it might be too warm and silted-in to support trout.

Fresh beaver cuttings—fat beaver pond trout may lurk just beyond the dam.

lodge an active one—are there fresh cuttings outside the lodge, telling you that the beavers have stocked the larder? An active lodge doesn't guarantee a productive beaver pond, but an inactive one tells you to move on. Take a look at the dam. If all of the sticks used to make the dam show signs of recent chewing, the pond may be a new one. Look carefully. Beavers will repair the dam regularly, and the sticks below the top layer may be old ones.

You want to be able to make a quick check at a beaver pond and then move along. You will often find a series of them as you head upstream, and one of them may be new and loaded with trout, and the rest barren. This is the hard way to do it. I have a friend who owns an airplane and flies over likely places each spring, making notes on a topo map. If he sees one that he hadn't noted before, it could be a gold mine. And do you think he shares them with the rest of us?

Big Rivers

By a big river I don't mean one that you have trouble casting across. In this book, a big river means one that makes you gasp when you first look at it, one that you'd rather cover by floating down with a drift boat than by walking along the bank.

Why aren't there any trout rivers the size of the lower Mississippi? A trout is mostly a creature of small rivers, those in upland areas, because of their narrow tolerance of temperatures. Rivers get larger as they flow through lowland areas. The lower in altitude you go, the less the water is influenced by groundwater springs, and the slower it flows, the warmer it gets and the less oxygen it will hold. This is why, outside of Alaska, northern Canada, and Argentina, most of our extremely wide trout streams are tailwater rivers of dams that release cold water from the bottom of deep reservoirs. In fact, two of the widest tailwater streams in North America flow through drainages that are too low in altitude and would not support trout without these artificial releases—the Delaware and the White in Arkansas. Many of our other famous large trout rivers, like the Bighorn and the Missouri in the Rockies, also owe their fame to dam releases.

Nearly all of these imposing rivers have a main current that moves faster than a trout prefers to live in or even faster than one will dart into for a morsel of food. Western float-fishing guides, probably the most experienced people at reading this kind of water, agree that fly fishermen hardly bother with the middle of an oversize river because the trout seldom are seen in this deep, fast water, and fly-fishing gear has trouble getting a presentation to a trout beneath twenty feet of raging current. But they disagree on whether the fish are even there.

Vern Bressler, born and raised on the Snake River drainage in Wyoming and Idaho, spends a lot of time floating the brawling South Fork of the Snake in Idaho. "I just don't think the fish hang in the center channel," he says. "There isn't any food, any protection there. Even the guys with heavy spinning gear don't catch any trout there."

In a river like this, with immense currents, you'll find most of the fish in the slicks along the bank. ***Photo by Bob White/Janice Fisher.***

Dave Kumlein is the proprietor of the Montana Troutfitters in Bozeman, Montana. He spends a lot of time on the lower Yellowstone River downstream of Yellowstone Park, one of the few exceptionally big trout streams that is not dammed. Dave believes "there's a few out there but nobody fishes for them." But he says that there are other places on the Yellowstone that are inhospitable for trout: "The outside of a fast bend, especially at the head, won't hold many fish. The current washes even the heaviest boulders away and the bottom is very uniform, without a place for the trout to hold."

Then you find a glaring exception that underscores the reason we find trout fishing unpredictable and tantalizing. Leigh Perkins, president of The Orvis Company and a man who has caught trout on six continents, told me a captivating tale of the Rio Grande in Argentina. The river, 100 yards wide, deep enough so the clear water looks almost black, and urgent in its rush downstream, gives up more trout, even to dry flies, from the middle of the river than from near the banks. How do the fish hold there? Where there is a steep drop-off in the river bed far below, giant upwellings form whirlpools on the surface. Apparently, these upwellings are so strong and predictable the trout can use them as they would rocks for supporting themselves in midstream. It would be fascinating to study these trout and find out if they rest and sleep in these upwellings, too, or if they spend part of the time on the bottom or near the banks.

If the middle of the river isn't a logical place to find trout, where do you look? It's hard to spot individual rocks in a river this size, as the water is too deep to allow the turbulence to be carried to the surface. Rather than looking for individual pieces of rock or log on the bottom, you have to look at the bigger picture. Western guides are unanimous in telling their clients to look for seams or "breaks" as they sometimes call them. A seam is any place fast water meets slow, and the best seams are usually

The inside of the seam, right where this boat is drifting, is a prime spot in a huge river. *Photo by Bob White/Janet Fisher.*

on the inside of a bend. Trout will lie in the smooth water adjacent to the riffled water. Dave Kumlein is more specific in that he often finds the most trout "quite a ways down the seam." The heads of the seams are often too swift to hold trout, unless you find some large boulders on the bottom. The faster the water is flowing, the farther down the seam the trout will be found.

We usually find seams in connection with a bend in the river, or if the channel of the river is straight, almost in the center of a river, just adjacent to a narrow band of exceedingly swift water. Yet in some wide, fast rivers, the bulk of the current is so fast that the seams on the outside of the fast water extend almost to the bank.

Bob Bachman, the biologist, was amazed the first time he fished the Bighorn. The trout he was used to observing lived and fed right out in the center of little Spruce Creek in Pennsylvania. "You wouldn't believe that place," he yelled to me over the phone after his first trip there. "Besides the gigantic fish, the environment and the behavior of the trout are totally different. The fast current extends right up to the bank, and even the slowest water, the stuff we normally call backwater, is fast enough to get the trout enough food. Every place you find a point along the bank with a little bay behind it, you'll find a pod of big trout."

In a river like this, where the current may be too swift for trout just a couple of yards from the bank, the water that holds them, in those backwaters along the bank, will usually be in the form of a whirlpool or eddy. The bank projection catches the current and whirls it around like an old man at a square dance. Remember, in your approach and in your presentation, that the fish closest to the bank may be facing downstream.

Vern Bressler is equally emphatic about the importance of side channels in giant trout streams. Where a river splits into many small streams, much of the energy and thus the velocity of the river is spent in splitting and winding around; also, the amount of water that is in contact with the banks increases, putting friction to work. "The fish will feed in the side channels before they will any place else," he says. "It's less work for them to hold in these areas of greatly reduced velocity, and besides being more trout here, they are more likely to come up for a dry fly. There is a tiny side channel on the Snake near my house that holds a six-pound cutthroat every year. Some years I catch him and others I don't."

If you've ever floated the Snake through Teton National Park you know how rare it is to see a six-pound cutthroat.

Finding trout in a side channel is virtually the same as in any other small- to medium-sized stream. Where in the main river, just a few yards away, the center of the river may be almost barren, here in the side channels the living is easier. Trout will live almost every place there is at least a foot of water with access to the main threads of current—which are even more important here because the rate at which food is brought to the fish is slower. I'd look a little closer at the downstream end of a side channel, before it rejoins the main river, than I would at the upper. The first half of a side channel is influenced more by the force of the current from the main part of the river, roaring into the little conduit like a rush-hour crowd into a subway where only one door works.

A side channel on the Madison. In contrast to the main river, where most of the trout will be close to the banks, you'll find the fish distributed throughout in a side channel.

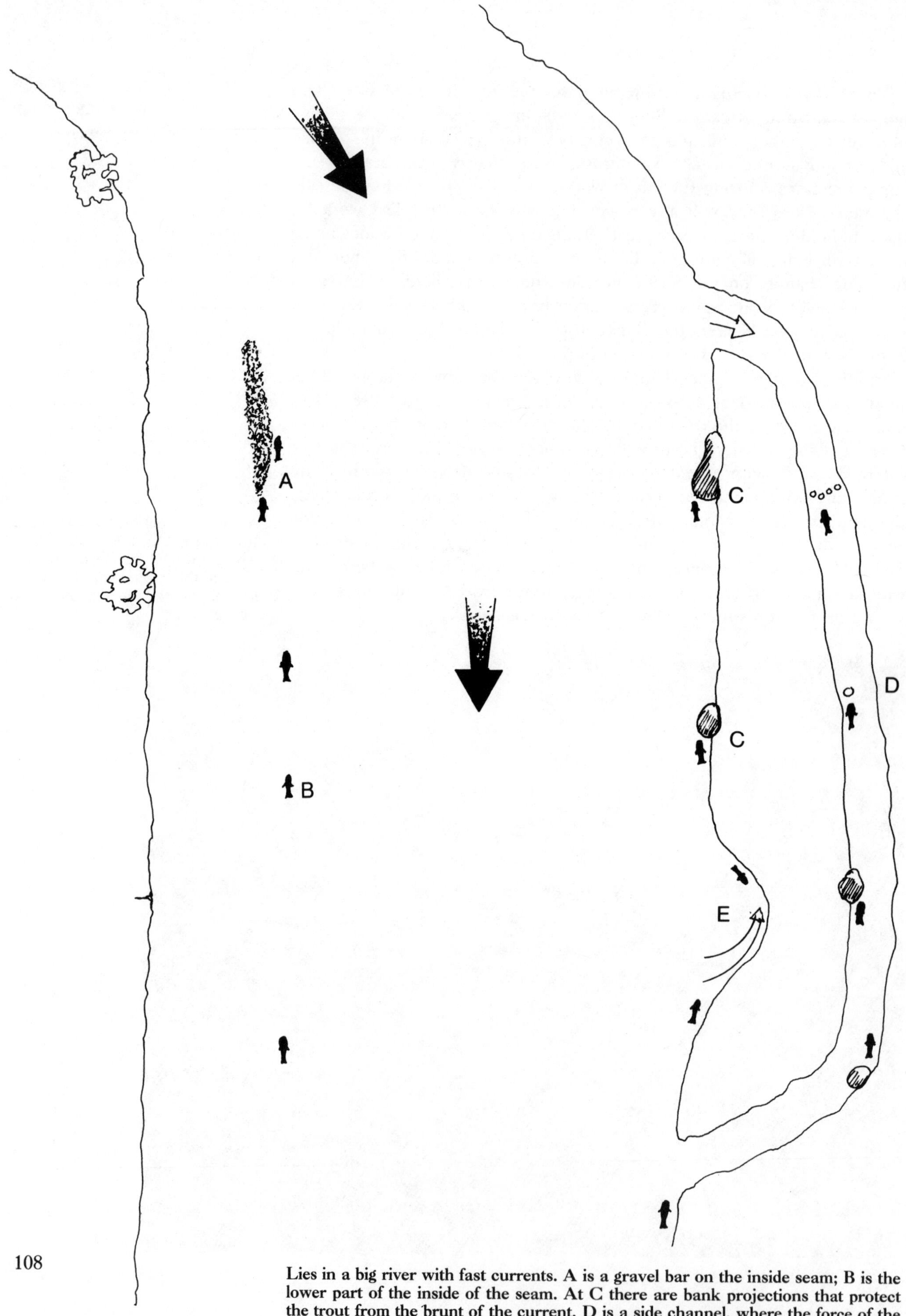

Lies in a big river with fast currents. A is a gravel bar on the inside seam; B is the lower part of the inside of the seam. At C there are bank projections that protect the trout from the brunt of the current. D is a side channel, where the force of the current is greatly reduced and fish will be found almost anywhere. E is a bay or backwater where trout will often be found surface feeding.

When fishing big rivers, especially when float fishing, you get lulled into a sense of routine and pound the banks with a hypnotic cadence. You know the fish are tucked in against the bank. But there are other places, not as easy to find but worth the effort. Bars, where deep water changes abruptly to shallow, may be as productive as the banks if you can find them. Dave Kumlein is constantly amazed to find trout "in three or four feet of water, right out in the open, where there is no overhead cover but a good steady flow of water." Where does he find these places? "All along the edges of gravel bars. In the Yellowstone, the heads of the bars are usually too shallow, but as soon as you get a quarter of the way down the bar you'll find trout right on the edge."

Finding bars is harder than fishing them, but if you can imagine where gravel would deposit during the spring floods, you have half the battle licked. Look for them on the inside of sharp bends. Bars will also be deposited in the center of a river, half-way down a pool or run, where the river suddenly widens from a relatively fast and narrow stretch into a "flat."

Where big rivers run through flat terrain and have correspondingly slow currents, the problem is different from that of many of the raging torrents in the West. Where the current in much of the river's channel is not fast enough to bring a steady food supply to the fish, they will bunch up in the faster currents—or they'll cruise for food. Examples of this kind of river would be the Delaware in the East and the Missouri in the West.

For example, it is senseless to try to read the water in the middle of a pool on the big Delaware below the confluence of its East and West branches. You will find trout in logical places at the heads of pools, in the waist-deep runs, studded with cobbles, that connect the aircraft-carrier-sized pools, and of course in the tails of pools. Here trout can find water in that one-foot-per-second velocity to rest in, yet find enough of this in proximity to faster water to get adequate food. But what happens when *all* of the water in the middle of a pool, even on the surface at the center of the river, is moving at less than two feet per second?

Cruisers. When the current is not sufficient to bring the food to them, trout will go after it, just as they would in a lake. After all, the same slow flow that is making it hard for the trout to find food is making it easier for them to get around without burning all of their valuable calories. Can you, looking at a pool that is so big you can't tell if that object at the other end is another fisherman or a dead tree, predict where the cruisers will be? Sometimes.

Trout don't cruise around a pool at random. They patrol an area, gliding upstream, sipping insects as they move, then they swim back downstream without eating and start the upstream feeding process again. I say "they" because you rarely see only one fish on patrol—their areas for cruising don't overlap but you might see three or four trout in an area that is twenty feet square and not see another trout for 100 feet in any direction. And trout will use the same places for this behavior for years.

Even though you can't perceive a current in a dead-still pool, it exists. Insects and other drifting foods may be concentrated in lanes. Look up to the head of the pool, find where the main part of the current is drifting, and imagine the current following the same trajectory through the pool. If

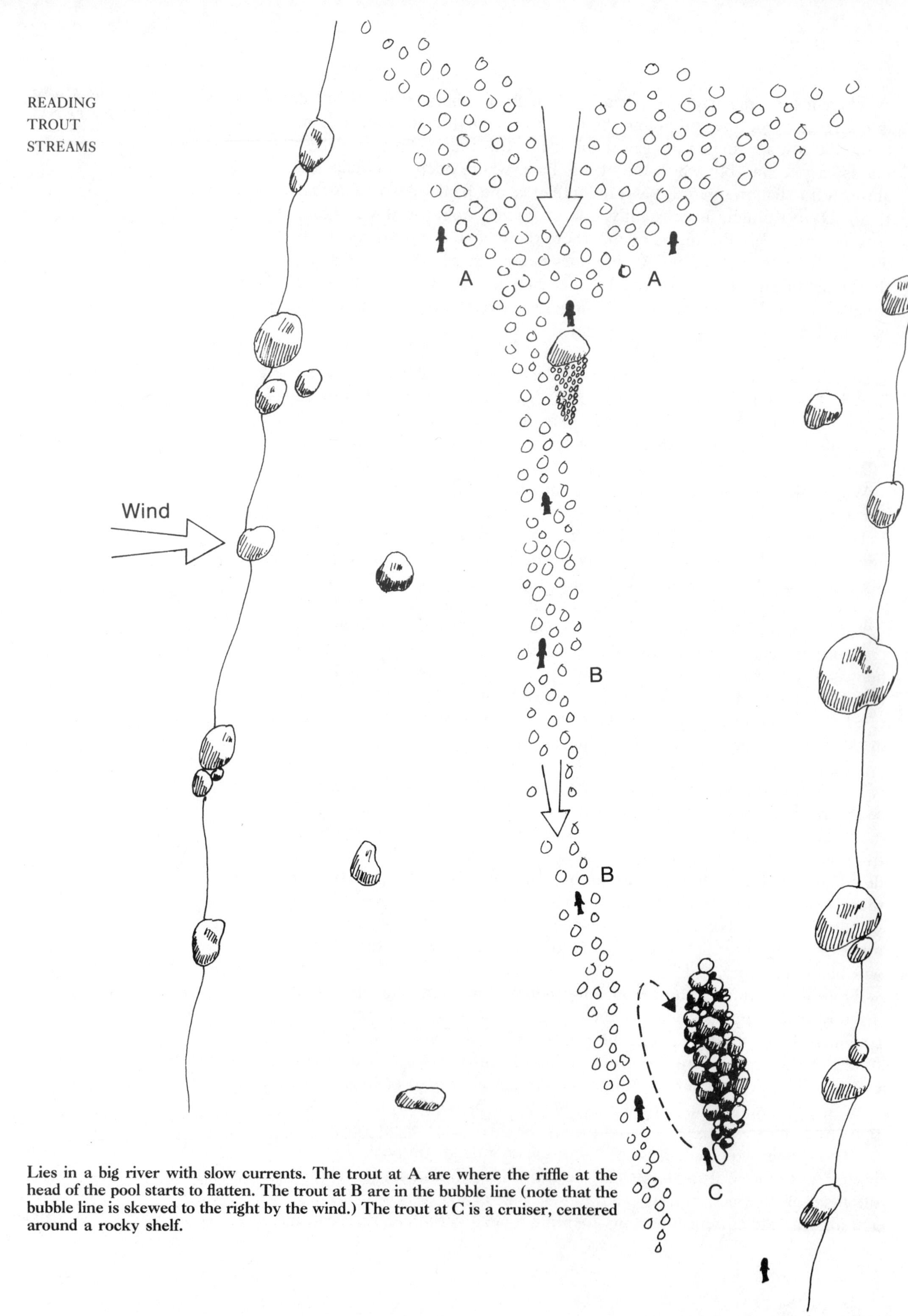

Lies in a big river with slow currents. The trout at A are where the riffle at the head of the pool starts to flatten. The trout at B are in the bubble line (note that the bubble line is skewed to the right by the wind.) The trout at C is a cruiser, centered around a rocky shelf.

The gravel bar below the island would be underwater at high water, but because it is on the inside of a sharp bend you might suspect its presence.

Art Lee in a cobble-studded run on the Delaware. Upstream and downstream are giant still pools with cruisers.

you look hard enough, bubbles and other debris may corroborate your ideas on where the food may be drifting—and it *is* drifting, no matter how still the surface of the pool may look.

Prevailing winds may also tip you off. Wind may be a stronger force in determining where food, especially surface food, drifts than currents. One large slow trout river that I've spent some time on flows north to south, and I always find the cruisers on the right side of the river as I'm looking upstream. Prevailing west winds blow the food there.

The bottom will also give you hints on where to find cruisers. Art Lee gives the best thoughts that I've heard on what to look for in an apparently lifeless pool: "Where the bottom is nondescript you won't find them. The typical place we find cruisers is where the depth of the water changes radically—I don't mean a great change in magnitude: from knee-deep to waist-deep will be enough. Generally there will be a line of stones that acts as a retaining wall, and on the inside of the edge it's often undercut. The trout will come up onto the shallow part much like bonefish coming onto a flat, and cruise along the edge. If danger threatens they don't have to bolt a long way for cover; they just slide back into the deep side of the edge."

You have some ideas on where to walk or drift or row. *Now* you can break that big river into little streams, fishing to the clues you've learned about in previous chapters.

7
Daily and Seasonal Changes

So far we've assumed that trout in streams don't move, and most of the time they don't. Every time they move they take risks. In some kinds of rivers, they move in daily rhythms but, fortunately for the fisherman, both the kinds of rivers and where the trout will move to are predictable. In all but the most stable rivers, those that never vary more than 10° in temperature throughout the year and only a few inches in flow, trout will change the positions they prefer over a twelve-month period.

In past chapters, we've assumed the rivers are "normal" for a trout stream in the height of the fishing season, when most of us see them. Water conditions are neither in drought nor in flood. This covers most of the season, from early May to July in the East and Midwest, and from mid-June (depending on altitude and the amount of runoff) to September in the West. And this "normal" water depends on weather that has not been unusually hot, cold, dry, or wet. Where are the fish earlier or later in the year, or when rivers are in flood or drought?

When trout change positions during the year, they are affected by three cues, two of them from the environment—current flow and temperature—and one from within, spawning urges. Here we're considering what will make a trout move from one rock, where he has lived for the past month, to another where he might spend the rest of the summer. Other factors that make trout move, like threats from predators or a sudden abundance of food in another part of the river, will only move them for a few hours.

Early Season

Let's start in early spring: no foliage on the trees, the water looks oily and cold and black, and the water is below 50°. At this temperature, a trout's metabolism is low, he has little inclination to feed—and he doesn't have to.

It's not even necessary for a trout to move during the winter, because his metabolism is so low that he is almost in suspended animation—and all his predators have hibernated or gone south for the winter. If the water warmed up to 40° and a couple of stonefly nymphs drifted right past his nose, he might have moved out of his tangle of roots for a brief meal, but he would have gone back to sleep as soon as the water cooled down.

Look for water that is over twenty inches deep. Anchor ice, a type of ice that forms on rocks on the bottom of the stream and at depths of twenty inches or less, can eliminate a trout's haven. A trout will seek out slow, deep water during the winter, because if he has to burn a lot of energy to move around and find another home, he'll die, as there is little food around during the winter to replace this lost energy. Regular surface ice can also form in slow pools, and when it breaks up in a thaw, it will scour all but the deepest pools.

In the first part of the season, *you* might think it's spring but the trout are still in winter quarters. Look for the slowest water in the river. There isn't much food drifting in the current, so a trout doesn't require that minimum flow of around two feet per second, and even if he fed he couldn't digest the food.

Slow water may not be as easy to find at this time of year, even in placid rivers. The Battenkill in its upper reaches reminds you of a channel full of molasses, but once you step into the river in the early season, you realize that trout will be found closer to the bank than to the middle of the river. And this is where we look, along the banks where a smooth "V" behind an obstruction on the bank signals slower water. The banks are especially valuable in the kinds of rivers that are deeper along the banks than in the middle, as opposed to rivers with wide gravel banks.

Another early-season location is in the seam at the head of a pool, especially on the inside of a curve—and better yet if there is an eddy or whirlpool. Anything that retards the downstream flow of a river and robs it of energy will create a place for a trout to live. At the head of Cairns' pool on the Beaverkill, perhaps the most intensively fished pool in the country, is a back eddy at the inside of a bend that most fishermen ignore. Yet Art Lee haunts that spot all winter and early spring, and seldom, unless it is excruciatingly cold, fails to find trout surface-feeding on midges there. The rest of the pool is often devoid of feeding fish.

This view of Schoharie Creek shows why trout seek deep water during the winter.

Although the Battenkill looks placid early in the season, the current is deceptively swift, so the fisherman is wise to place his fly close to the bank. The slick along the bank indicates slower water.

Look for places where the sun will warm the water. A flat, shallow middle of a pool will be warmer and more comfortable to the trout than a narrow, deep chute. Besides, the flow of the river in the flat will be spread out, so the current will be slower. And a piece of stream that runs through a meadow may not hold more trout than canyon water in April, but the water will be warmer in the meadow and more trout will be feeding.

Don't forsake pocket water in early spring. All that turbulence and white water is current energy being dissipated, and many slow pockets are sprinkled between the rocks and white water. One March, my friend Alan DeNicola decided to brave bitter air temperatures to try a stream in New York State that is open all year long. I must have been pretty confident when I advised him to try the deeper pools and slow backwaters. And Alan was magnanimous when he came back with a snapshot of the large brown trout he pulled from a stretch of shallow pocket water.

Most trout fishermen know that trout will congregate around the mouths of springs and spring-fed tributaries in the dog days of summer. Did you know these spots can be equally attractive to trout in the early season? Springs are cold in the summer because they come out of the ground at a constant temperature, year-round. This temperature is close to the mean annual temperature at a given latitude, which in most trout areas of the United States is between 45° and 50°. When the water temperature of a trout stream is only 39°, but the mouth of spring-fed tributary is pouring in water at a balmy 50°, you can bet the trout will gang up for many yards below the mouth of the trib.

You can identify spring-fed tributaries because they will usually run clear in the spring, when rain and snow-melt-fed tribs carry a heavy load of mud and debris. Springs that enter the bed of the river are harder to find now than in August, when you didn't mind thrusting your arm into the river to get a thermometer near the bottom. If you didn't find any springs last summer, don't worry. An easier time to find springs is in January, and you won't have to leave your heated car.

Wait until the morning temperatures get down to below 0° Fahrenheit and take an early-morning ride along the river. It should be so cold and still that you'll want to go back to bed. Now look for steam rising from discrete places in the river. Every spot that looks a little smoky should be marked on a map, because these are your spring holes. And they will be the best places to find trout when the water is below 50° or above 70°.

Side channels in rivers, even if they are only pressure valves for spring floods and are dry the rest of the year, can be productive places to fish when the water is cold. The water in these channels will be slower, shallower, and warmer than water in the main channel. The first time I fished the Battenkill, before I lived in Vermont, I got to the river at one of those early-May floods when even the guys in the fly shops, normally hotbeds of optimism, tell you to give up and go home. But I had to try the famous Battenkill. Walking to the river by a little side channel that was obviously dry in normal years because of the young aspen trees growing in the center of it, I saw a rise. And then several rises. The channel was full of brook trout that had moved out of the river to get away from the flood. When I moved to Vermont years later I remembered that side channel

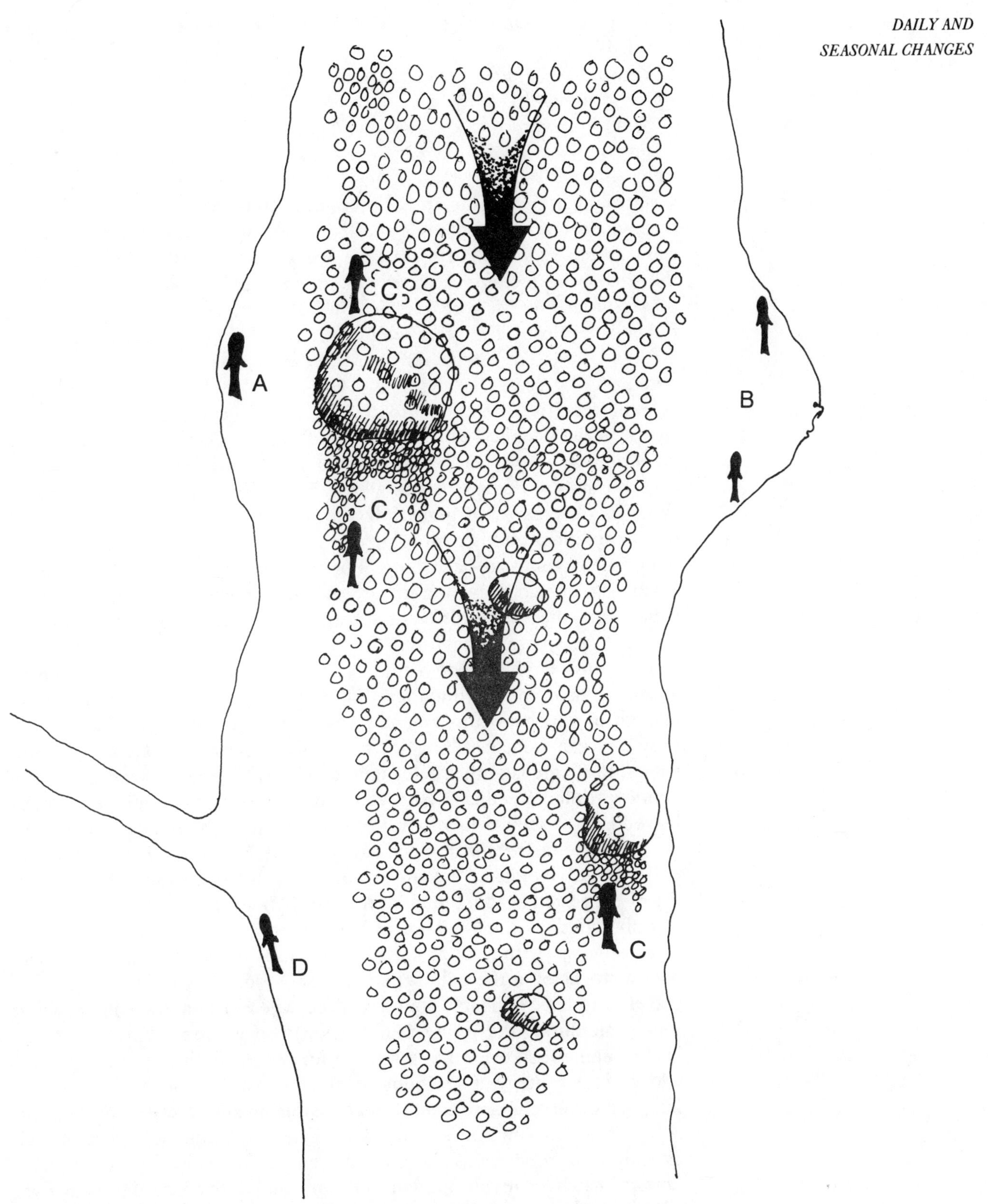

Early-season lies. The trout will be found along the banks at A, near backwaters at B, protected by large rocks at C, or below the mouth of warmer spring-fed tributaries, D.

and planned to use it as an ace-in-the-hole when the rest of the river was unfishable.

A gravel bar built up over the mouth of the channel and it hasn't had water in it since I've lived in Vermont.

Now I'm going to throw you a couple of curves. Will that temperature business I've been telling you so confidently always predict how active trout will be? In rare circumstances the rules don't hold. One March, I was looking at two spring creeks that run into Agency Lake in Oregon, on the property of the fabulous Take-It-Easy Ranch. There was two feet of snow on the ground and the water temperature was in the low forties. Yet the trout were feeding as eagerly as trained seals. Randy Sparacino, the owner of the ranch, told me that the trout in his spring creeks don't follow the rules. The water temperatures in his creeks never get above 50°, and the trout are healthy and perfectly acclimated to these temperatures.

Some strains of rainbow trout and all subspecies of cutthroat trout spawn in the spring. Their behavior and the places you'll find them may be different from what I talked about in the preceding paragraphs, at least during the actual spawning period, which only lasts a few weeks. When is this spawning period? It varies with the species, altitude, and water conditions and is hard to predict unless you know the history of the river you're going to be fishing. For instance, cutthroats in the Snake River system start spawning in early April, whereas cutthroats in Yellowstone Park (they are a different subspecies and live at a higher altitude) may still be spawning in July.

The most likely place to find rainbows or cutthroats near spawning season is in or near tributaries. They don't need much water, barely enough in which to turn around. Any river or brook that runs into the Pacific Ocean from Los Angeles to southern Alaska, or one that is connected to a large lake that holds rainbows, may also have silvery migratory rainbows called steelhead. But we're going to stick to nonmigratory rainbows that live their whole lives in rivers, because the philosophy of finding and fishing for anadromous salmonids is a subject that requires an entire book. (I've listed a couple of excellent books on this subject in my list of suggested reading at the end of this book.)

Tributaries. Just any tributary? No, rainbows prefer to spawn in clear, rocky streams, with a lot of gravel in the stream bed. If you find a small pool with gravel in the tail of the pool and a foot or two of water over the gravel, you have probably found a place where a rainbow will spawn at some time during the spring. Rainbows will spawn in streams that go dry in the summer, so even if you know a feeder stream is intermittent, take a look. This strategy of spawning in streams that don't hold water all year long makes more adaptive sense than just using all the water that is available. These intermittent streams don't harbor any aquatic predators such as sculpins or predaceous water beetles and their larvae. The young rainbow fry hatch relatively unmolested, and drop back into the main river before the water drops in the summer.

If the main river has a lot of clean gravel for spawning, rainbows may spawn right in the main channel. Look for them in the tails of pools or at the top or bottom of riffles. The important thing to remember is that for spawning success they must have a strong current, so they will be found in much swifter water in the early spring than browns, brookies, and fall-spawning strains of rainbows—mainly those strains of rainbows that were recently stocked or have hatchery genes in their pedigree.

Cutthroats also move into tributaries to spawn but they are less concerned about getting back into the river. Many of the cutthroats that move into small tributaries of the Snake near Jackson Hole in April decide they like the living there and will remain in the tribs until September. These aren't juveniles, either—many of them will tip the scale at four or five pounds.

As an aside, does it make biological sense to restrain from fishing over trout that are spawning? That is a question only you can answer, but consider this: Mortality in trout populations after they reach spawning age, other than fishing mortality, is extremely low. If you kill a female brown trout in June, you've killed a spawner full of eggs just as sure as if you had killed her in October. What about pestering the trout when they're spawning? There are usually two or three males to each female on a redd, and the males beat each other up constantly. It will invariably be the male that takes your fly, and if you kill it another male will take his place quickly. If you release him, he'll be back scrapping with the other males in an hour. Is it any more perverted to catch, play, and release a trout when he is spawning than when he is eating?

As the water temperature warms into the mid-forties, trout begin to move into places where they have access to the faster currents that will bring them drifting food. Their metabolisms begin to increase rapidly, as does the availability of insects. Currents slow down so there are more places for the trout to feed. All the pieces of the puzzle come together at the same time. Now we're into the heart of the season, the circumstances described in previous chapters.

Floods

Once a river gets into mid-season stability, what happens when a rainstorm raises its level? Do the trout move into different places because of the increase in depth and velocity? Unfortunately, most of the time they don't. I say unfortunately because the trout stay put; but it's harder for us to get our flies to them, since they usually can't see a floating fly or insect, making dry-fly fishing difficult or futile. And it is a lot tougher getting your wet fly or nymph or streamer down to where the fish can see it.

When the water rises, a trout that is already sitting in an area of reduced velocity doesn't have to move. Water running over his head and to the sides gets a lot faster, but dead spots and cushions around objects don't change, so he sits tight and gorges on the increased food supply riding the current. This is why even the most vicious floods do little harm to an adult trout population. Young-of-the-year trout, those four inches long and less, can be decimated by a severe flood, though, and the fishing two or three years later may suffer as a result.

A river in obvious flood. Most of the trout will sit tight and wait for high water to recede.

By looking at the alders along the bank, you can tell that the river is in flood, and you can also figure out how much higher than normal the level is by seeing how far the alders extend under water.

I should say *most* trout don't move—but some, those living in gentle riffles or seams on the inside or outside of bends, will move into the slicks along the banks to get out of the angry currents in the middle of the river. Also, trout living behind submerged rocks may need to pull back into the focal point to get out of the increased buffeting of the turbulence immediately behind the rock. The trout lying along the banks will be the easiest to catch, because they will be in water that is clear and shallow compared to the water in the center of the river, and more likely to see your fly. Trout will also move to these two places in tailwater rivers that are used to generate power, where the water will rise and fall daily, sometimes with surprising speed.

How do you tell when a river is higher than normal, cueing you to look in these locations? The easiest place to check is along the banks. Many kinds of streamside foliage will grow out of the water in the riparian zone, but their leaves will grow up and out of the water, not back into it. If the leaves of any foliage along the banks are underwater, you have a river that is in flood. By looking carefully, you can even tell how high above normal the river is by how much water is covering the lowermost leaves.

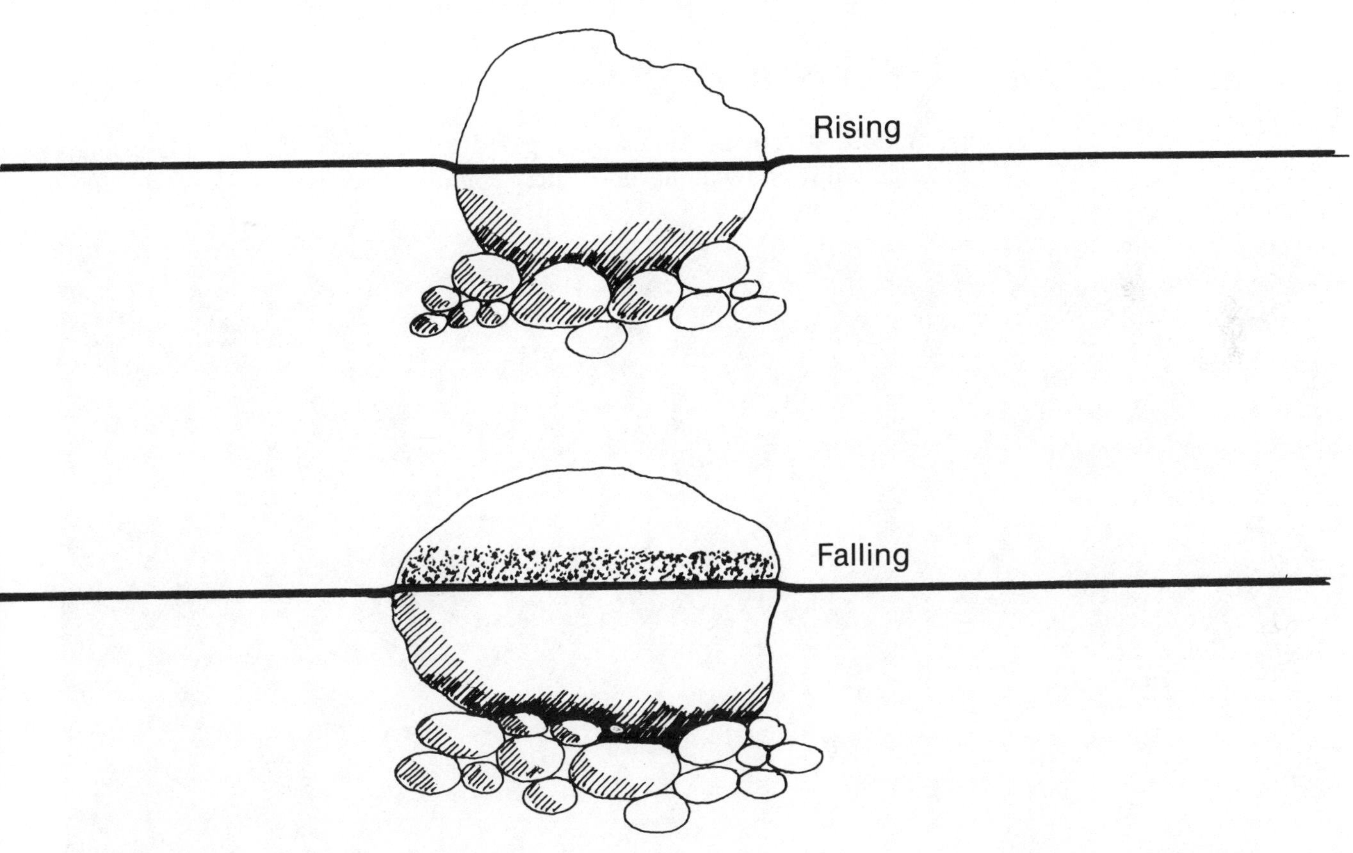

Rising water. The meniscus curves down onto the dry rock.
Falling water. The top of the rock is wet and the meniscus curves up to the rock.

I've also been able to tell if an unfamiliar river is in flood by turning over rocks in the shallows. Start right next to the bank. Turn over a few rocks and look for any kind of aquatic life—caddisfly cases, mayflies, stoneflies, or even plain old aquatic slime. If the undersides of the rocks are completely clean, move toward the center of the river and turn over some more rocks. When you start finding some type of underwater life you've found the high-water mark of normal flow.

You can also tell if the water level is either rising, staying the same, or falling by looking at rocks in the river or objects along the bank. If there is a wet line above the surface of the water on rocks that are in the river, or if the plants or debris along the banks have a still-wet coating of silt for a few inches above the water line, you know the river is dropping. Another way is to look at the meniscus of the water in relation to a rock in the river. If the meniscus curves upward to the rock, the water is dropping; if it curves slightly downward, the water is rising or stable. I know of no way of telling for certain if a river is rising slowly, but I've heard of fishermen on tailwater rivers putting a five-dollar bill on top of a rock that is a foot or so above the water. This keeps their eyes on fast-rising flows, and when the bill is in danger of floating away it's time to get out of the river.

The Late Season

A trout stream in August, compared to the same river in May, looks like an old friend who has lost thirty pounds. The framework is still there

but the substance has changed. The most obvious change is there are fewer places for a trout to live. Pocket-water areas and riffles that were full of trout in the spring may be only six inches deep. In mid-season, almost every place in the river had the potential to hold trout—all but the slowest backwaters and the shallowest edges. Now the places that hold trout have shrunken and you may find entire stretches of river barren, while certain locations will host pods of trout, all crowded into a small area.

Can we predict where these places will be? You bet. The first consideration is that trout in a small stream have to be more mobile throughout the season than those in a big river, so the smaller the stream the more walking you may have to do. In a study comparing a large Scottish salmon

The head of a pool on the Housatonic in April (left) and in August (bottom). Since it is a gentle riffle, the fishermen will find trout scattered throughout in April but if they return in August they should concentrate at the head of the riffle.

river with small streams in the same area, the entire bed of the salmon river was still covered with water at one-eighth of the mean annual discharge of the river. The small streams began to contract in width at one-half the mean annual discharge—and at one-eighth annual discharge only one-third of the river bed was wet.

The dog days of summer conspire against trout. Not only are a lot of their lies dry or exposed to predators for lack of depth, but water temperatures and thus the amount of oxygen in the water are reduced, and the flow of the river is reduced to the point where only a narrow band of the stream channel will bring enough food to a drift-feeding trout.

We'll look at flow first. Remember that trout prefer to lie in water that moves at about one-half foot per second but they need water running at two feet per second or more at close hand to get enough food. During times of low water, there may be only a narrow band of water that runs near two feet per second, and it will be wherever the line of the main current flows through a pool. Watch for the line of bubbles through the pool. If this line runs through the center of the pool, there will be a migration of the trout that were living near the banks toward the center. Many times, the main current will flow along one bank, usually the deeper one, and the fish will be there both for the food supply and the protection that the deep water and the bank provide.

The head of a pool, where the water is running faster, is one of the places where trout move when the flow is reduced. The head has other attractions as we'll see later; but not all the trout in a pool will move to the head. Those in the middle of the pool, where flow is the slowest, will often take up cruising to get enough food. Whether they will be cruising or drift feeding will depend if they can find current that runs close to two feet per second, but I can tell you from experience that trout in the middle of a pool at low water will be "podded up" or concentrated in discrete locations. Where the bottom is mostly sand or small rocks, they will center around some type of cover they can run to if danger threatens in the shallow water.

In the Battenkill, there is a stretch of river called "The Jungle" that is straight for 100 yards, without riffles or other distinguishing features, and relatively shallow. The bottom is sand. During August, when the diminutive mayflies we call the Tricos are hatching, nearly every trout in the river will be rising, so you can get a fair idea of where they are living. Every place there is a log across the river, or where a bush hangs out over the water, you'll find a dozen trout rising in an area the size of a car. Once you've spooked the whole pod, as I invariably do, you look up the river for the next bunch. It may be over fifty feet before you see another bunch of fish rising—and there won't be a trout in between.

You hear talk about trout living near overhanging trees and streamside brush during the summer because "there aren't as many aquatic insects available so the trout are hanging out where terrestrial insects fall into the water." A trout living under an overhanging willow might get fractionally more of the ants falling into the water from the tree; but anything that falls into the water near the banks is drawn into the center of the river, and rides the same currents as the tiny mayflies, caddisflies, midges, and other debris that forms the soup we call drift. The trout near the trees may be there for the additional protection from ospreys and kingfishers, or because they can see better when looking from the shade into the sun—or perhaps the main threads of current flow under the tree.

Seldom does reduction of flow alone determine where trout will be found during low water. The lowest water usually occurs during the hottest part of the summer, so trout will move both toward the main line of current and to where temperatures are lower or there is more oxygen in the water. (Remember that more oxygen can be put into the water two ways: physically by its interaction with the air in riffles or white water, or by cooling off because oxygen is more soluble in cold water.)

The faster water in the main-current flows will have more dissolved oxygen because as water stagnates it loses oxygen to the surrounding air. But there are other places trout will move to when they begin gasping for air. The natural place is anywhere you see white water, as the bubbles that cause the white mean that water is mixing thoroughly with the air. Stick your thermometer in the water in the main flow at midday. If the water temperature is near 70° and you have suspicions that daytime temperatures have been this high for more than a day, trout will start to move to where there is more oxygen in the water. Fish in a long pool will move to the head; the warmer the water gets, the closer to the white water they will be. In a piece of pocket water, the trout will begin to pull in from the edges of the current to the center, where there is a stronger flow and thus more white water.

An even more vivid example of the effect of high temperatures on trout is their migration toward cooler water. Apparently, a lowering of the water temperature 10° will overshadow any amount of mixing that can occur in white water. In the Housatonic, a tailwater river that suffers from high temperatures almost every August, trout will gang up around the mouth of cool feeder streams, and tumbling white water just yards away will be barren. In fact, the trout get so concentrated around these feeders that fishing is prohibited by law within 100 feet of their mouths.

Trout may migrate upstream in their search for cooler water, since the headwaters of a river are normally colder than the lower reaches, unless cold feeder streams or springs change the character of the lower river. I cannot prove this but in a lot of the rivers I fish the upper reaches seem to hold more fish as the season progresses, long before trout should be moving to spawn.

Because feeder streams are cooler—being smaller, more shaded, and closer to sources of groundwater than bigger rivers—trout will be attracted to them at times of high water temperatures. Even a couple of degrees will move trout from one end of a pool to another. If the water in a river is 70° and a trib coming in at the head of the right side of the pool is 66°, trout will be lined up along the right side of the pool for twenty feet below the mouth of the smaller stream. If the trib's temperature is 60°, the fish might be stacked in below the mouth for twice that distance.

The influx of cold water may not be as obvious. A friend had been having great luck in a pool that never looked appealing to me. One hot August morning, I was not seeing any trout in favorite pools, so I climbed

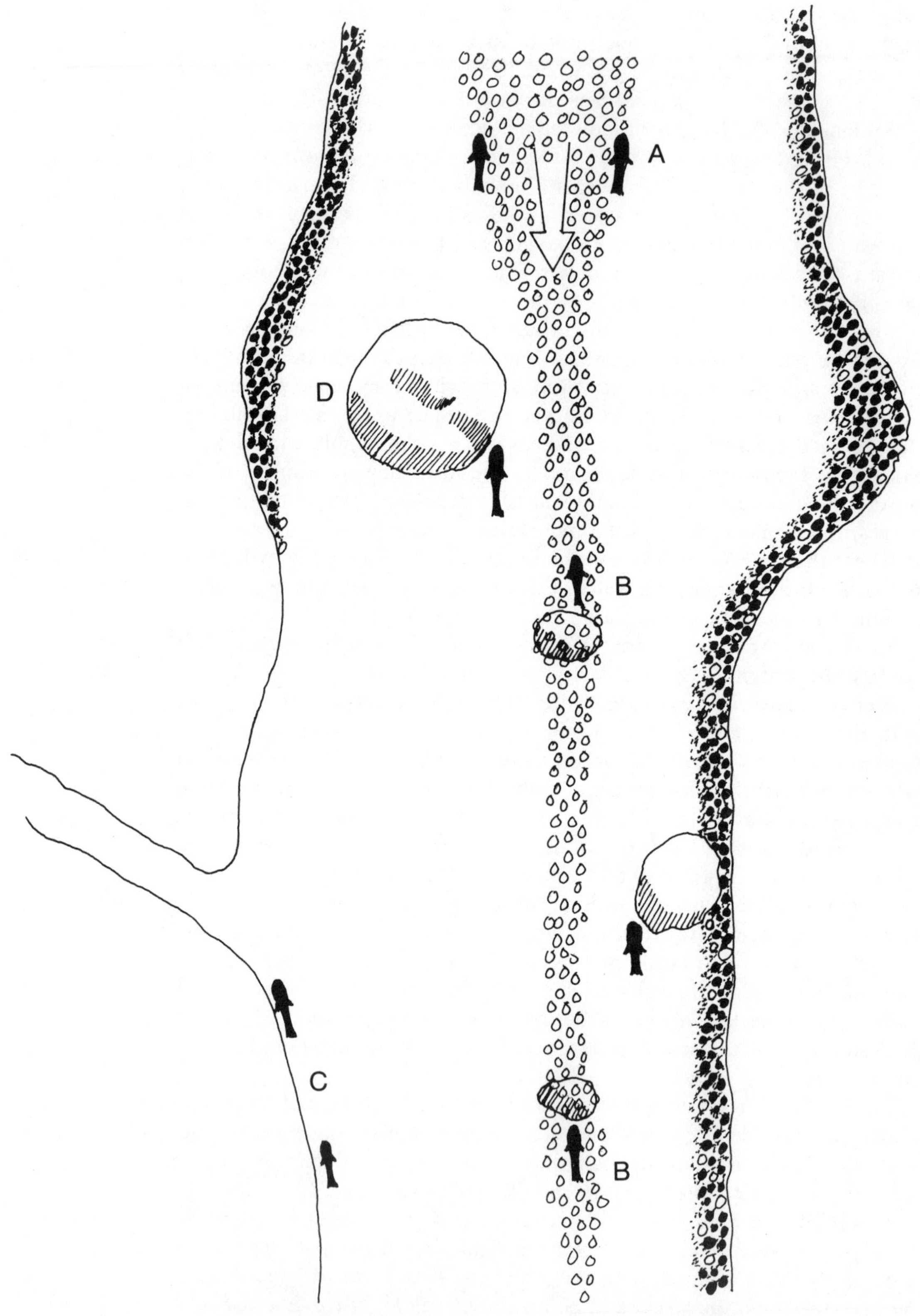

Late-season lies. The trout have moved to the head of the pool for more oxygen (A), into the bubble line (B), or below colder spring-fed tributaries (C). Note that the early-season lies along the bank are now dry, and the left side of the rock at D no longer offers a steady food supply.

This sign is posted around the mouths of cool tributaries on the Housatonic; it prohibits fishing during the hot months, when trout are so concentrated in these places they can be foul-hooked easily.

down the bank to the edge of his pool. A wave of cool air hit me like a slap in the face. Then I heard a soft tinkling sound. Three springs were hidden where the steep bank fell down to the river, and the water upstream of the springs was 72°—and thirty feet below it was 67°.

Here was one clue: where a river flows up against a steep bank, frequently you will find a spring coming out of a fault in the side of the hill. If the steep bank is made of ledgerock you can count on it—the base of the ledgerock will hold some nice trout when the weather gets hot. The water may be a mere trickle that isn't visible from across the river, but even a flow of 50° water that wouldn't fill a thimble in five minutes is enough to save a trout's life when the water in a river is over 75°.

Don't overlook the mouth of a dry feeder stream as a source of cool water. There might not be any water on the surface but below the dry gravel of the stream bed—somewhere—is groundwater that is seeping into the river.

Some springs come into a river without any hints. These you can find by using your thermometer, dipping it into various places in the river bed, but it's probably easier to wade "wet," without waders, letting your legs do the work while you look for rises. Also, be on the lookout for mist that rises from a particular place in the river on a hot, muggy night. The cool water will condense the moisture in the warm air above.

Along with a gradual migration toward the headwaters in the summer because of warm temperatures, brown and brook trout, fall spawners, will begin to feel the effects of their hormones. This migration can be across the pool or it can be for twenty miles. In a study done in Michigan, it was found that brook trout searched out areas that were 80 percent groundwater or spring water mixed with 20 percent surface water, which is the stuff that makes up most of the flow in a trout stream. Browns were less picky, in that they liked a 50-50 mix of groundwater to surface water. This study agrees with the observations of most fishermen—that brown

A ledgerock spring that attracts big trout throughout the year. It offers warm water in the early spring and cool water in the summer. Even later in the year, when the spring is not obviously dripping, cold water will still enter the bed of the river underground.

trout often spawn right in the main channel of a river, whereas brookies will move into the upper limits of feeder streams or to the mouths of springs.

Brown trout may also live in parts of rivers that have little groundwater flow, like the lower reaches of many of our big trout rivers, or in lakes, where they are unable to spawn. Because they are close relatives of Atlantic salmon, you would expect them to return to the spot where they were born to spawn, and they do. In big Rocky Mountain rivers like the Madison and Yellowstone, the yearly migrations of brown trout to spawn are well known, and fishermen chase them with big nymphs and streamers until painful snowstorms or closed seasons drive them off the river.

Besides the proper mix of water, fall spawning trout also need the right size and quantity of gravel. In some rivers they will move into side channels to find the right kind of gravel. Dave Kumlein gave me a succinct answer to where and when he looks for big brown trout in the fall, particularly in the Yellowstone River.

"When we have our first storms near the autumnal equinox, in late September, after the water drops I look for them in the last third of a pool, in gravel runs that have three or four feet of water over them. If you find the tail of a pool with golf-ball-sized rocks you'll find brown trout in the fall. If the gravel is any finer it gets compacted, and the eggs won't be able to fall down through the cracks, where they are protected."

How's that for a precise description?

Daily Movements

In some streams, trout move around in the course of a day. The distance they can or will move around in a river depends on the current speed—trout in a brawling piece of pocket water will not move unless driven from their positions by low water or spawning urges; trout in a sloughlike spring creek will move around all day long. In between is the typical freestone stream where, at certain times of the year, trout will move from areas of cover to more exposed lies to feed.

Trout never move in a random or aimless manner, unless they are sick or just-released hatchery fish. When they cruise a pool, they always follow a stylized pattern, centered around a piece of cover like a submerged shelf or a log. The trout swim upstream, sipping insects at regular intervals as if the journey, not feeding, was their real purpose. When they reach a position that has significance only to a trout, they slide downstream to the starting point, seldom feeding on the way back.

Trout often cruise in spring creeks. While they may cruise anywhere in a spring creek, because food is so abundant it is all around, the time of day they do so can be predicted. In Letort Spring Run in Pennsylvania, you see cruising early in the morning, before the sun hits the water. Trout are out looking for sow bugs and scuds, two freshwater crustaceans that are so abundant a handful of watercress will yield thousands of squirming arthropods. When the sun comes up, the fish will gently slink back into the deep channels between the weeds.

Yet if you fish one of the many spring creeks in Montana, Wyoming, or Idaho, it is often a waste of time to get on the river before ten in the morning. If you get there earlier, the trout will be tucked into the weeds, not feeding and not interested in any of your best flies.

The difference between these two spring creeks is temperature. Springs reflect the average mean temperature of the location they are in, thus springs in Pennsylvania are warmer than springs in Montana. The metabolisms of the trout in Montana don't get them moving until sun warms the water.

Trout cruise in freestone rivers as well as spring creeks; you generally see this in the bigger pieces of water. The determining factor, though, is current. When the velocity of the current gets down below one foot per second, trout will move around for their food. Sometimes this cruising lasts all day long and on other days trout will cruise only for a few minutes, at the height of an insect hatch.

The kind of daily movement you see commonly, that occurs in moderate or even fast currents, is a jump from one feeding site to another. Some fishermen talk about "resting lies" and "feeding lies" as though the fish spent part of the day feeding and part of it sleeping. Behavioral

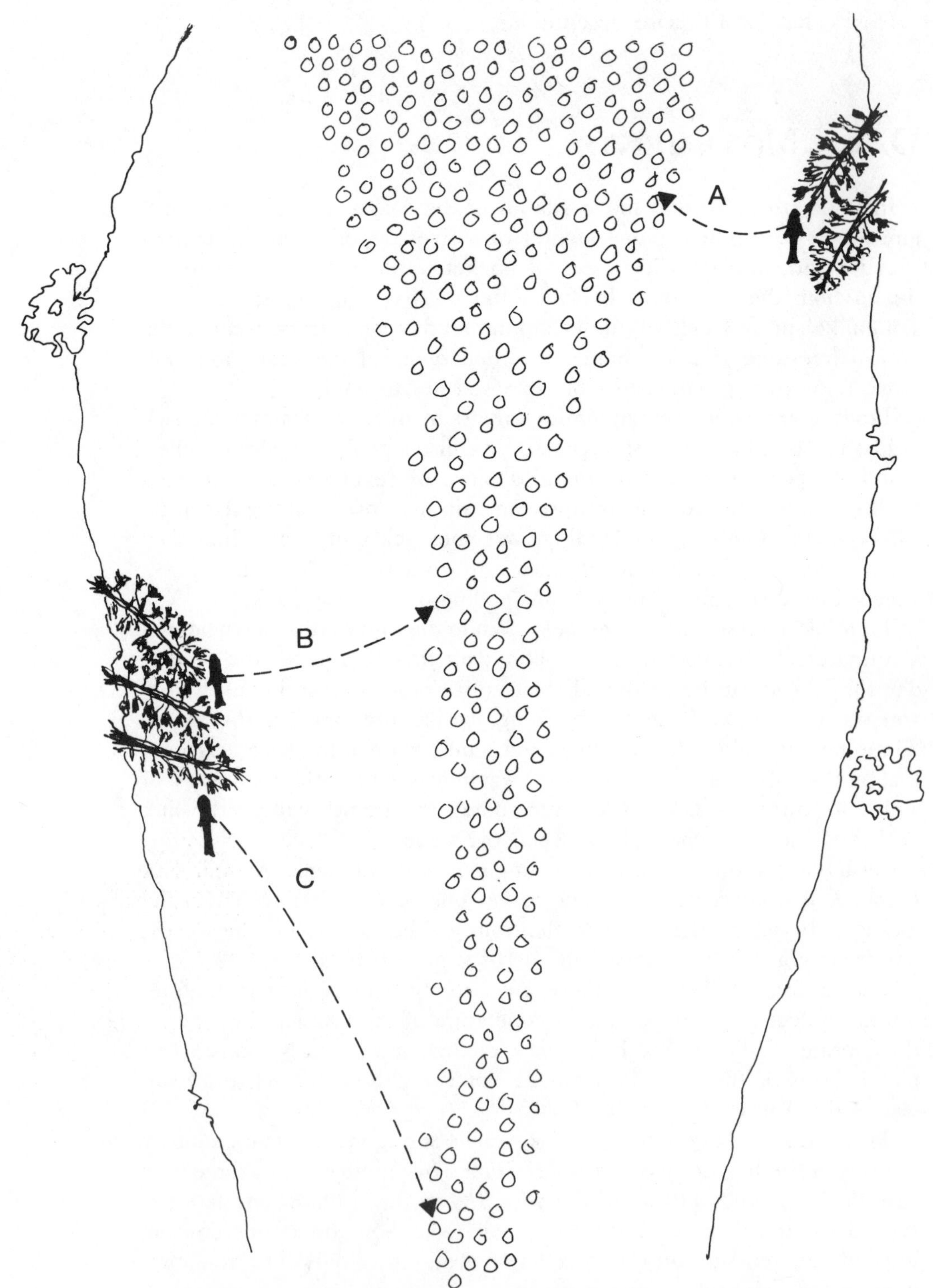

Daily movements of trout in a river with heavy fishing or canoe pressure. During a heavy hatch, usually in the evening, the trout will move from protection into the head of the pool (A), the edge of the central current (B), or into the tail (C).

scientists like Bob Bachman observe trout feeding all day long, unless they are frightened into sanctuaries. The fish will move from one site to another, but they feed at both locations. Apparently, the trout sense that one site has more food than the other. Bachman spent 3,000 hours watching trout in the tail of a pool in Pennsylvania's Spruce Creek; not once did he see a fish from the tail of the pool move to the head, or vice versa.

On the other hand, Leonard Wright, writing in *The Ways of Trout*, documented brown trout in a pool in a relatively infertile Catskill river (Bachman's fish were also brown trout but Spruce Creek is uncommonly fertile) moving fifty feet or more to the head of a pool to feed in the evening—and several nights later the same trout were in the tail of the pool! The amount of food is probably the determining factor in this kind of movement, as the trout in Spruce Creek didn't *have* to move to get sufficient food. How Wright's fish knew which end of the pool to feed in I don't know, but the answer would be fascinating.

Usually a move of this type happens in the evening, after the sun leaves the water. It comes at a time when daylight is rapidly waning, but also when insect activity escalates. The kind of movement you often see is from a deep run along a bank, where there is protection for the trout in the form of both depth and overhanging brush. The trout may be feeding all day in there, but when insects blanket the water in the evening, the fish appear to sense that food is easier to get out in the center of the river, where the main flow of drift is found. If the pool has a deep bank on one side and is shallower in the middle, if the current is moderate to slow they will slide out toward the center of the river.

They will also move to the head of a pool if it is the kind of head that simpers into a pool, without a great rush of water. A gentle riffle allows fish to slip upstream easily and feed for an hour, where a great plume of water would make it impractical, for trout must struggle against the current.

On the big tailwater rivers in the Rocky Mountains, like the Bighorn or the Missouri, some trout will use the edges of the fast, deep currents for protection. In these rivers, trout will move *toward* the bank when a heavy hatch of insects blankets the water. It is far easier for the fish to move into backwaters near the bank and reap the harvest of an easy meal without having to tussle with the current. And unlike other rivers you may fish, they will usually move during the day, because in these rivers most of the insect hatches take place during the day.

I'm saving the best for last—the tail. I had always known that trout, usually the largest ones in a pool, would sometimes feed in the shallowest part of the tail, right out in the middle, because it is easier to suck up drifting food there than anyplace else in the pool. What I didn't realize was the distance trout would travel for choice morsels of food.

A couple of years ago, my wife, Margot, and I happened to be on the Beaverkill at the height of the Green Drake spinner fall. This spinner, known locally as the Coffin Fly, is gigantic—a size 6 or 8—and falls in suffocating numbers at dusk. The spinners flying upstream look like the old newsreel pictures of B-29s leaving Okinawa for the Japanese mainland. Trout go absolutely insane, comparable to the way they behave for the *Hexagenia* hatch in the Midwest or the salmonfly hatch in the West.

We were fishing with Art Lee and his friend Galen Mercer, who both haunt the Beaverkill every night. Art has never steered me wrong on this river but this time I had doubts. He led us both out to the tail of one of the huge pools below the junction of the Little Beaverkill and the Willowemoc. Not in the good water at the far bank, where the water slowed and deepened, where I *knew* the best trout were. No, right out in the middle, where the water was up to the middle of my calf and I could see every stone on the bottom. Upstream, I could see all the other fishermen in the pool, standing in line facing that seductive deep bank like a row of sentries. They kept looking back at us, standing all alone in that shallow, lifeless tail. Boy, did I feel stupid.

"Just hang on, don't be impatient," Art said. "As soon as the sun gets off the water the fish will move out from the bank and hang in behind each one of those Vs that mark a rock on the bottom." And they did. Big trout, eighteen- to twenty-inchers that were not there when the sun was on the water. The bank, the nearest deep water, was seventy-five feet away. I had visions of those huge trout slinking between the legs of the army of fishermen upstream, leaving them fishing over vacant quarters and me in the catbird seat.

The next time I spoke with Bob Bachman, I asked him how he explained those fish, because Bob is a big proponent of the "trout don't move far to feed" school. Were those trout really coming from almost 100 feet away, I asked him, right out in the open in shallow water. "I'll bet they were," he said. "They most likely even *anticipate* the hatch every night once it gets in full swing. The big trout come out one evening looking for minnows and find those big drakes out in the open—nice easy pickings. There are more flies and they're easier to get in the tail of the pool, so the next night the fish come out looking for them."

The clincher to this phenomenon of large trout moving a long way to feed in a tail of a pool was something Rusty Gates told me about. Biologists in Michigan did a telemetry study of a large trout, attaching a sensor to a nineteen-inch brown. The fish lived in an impenetrable brush pile, and after dark it would move 100 yards to the tail of a pool to feed, apparently on minnows and crayfish. But a few times, when there was an extremely heavy hatch during the day, the fish would slink down to *the same place, 100 yards away,* to feed on insects drifting on the surface.

8
Interactions

What besides currents, water level, temperature, and food may affect where trout are found in streams? The interactions that first come to mind, like juggling for position between different species of trout and different sizes of trout within one species, have little impact on where trout live. A less obvious factor, the activities of fishermen and boaters on moving water, has a greater consequence on where you will find them.

Differences Between the Species

It's easy to stereotype the places you'll find the different species of trout, and for generations parents have told their children that rainbows like fast water and browns prefer the slower neighborhoods. This time the old fables are, for the most part, true.

Rainbows *are* creatures of fast water. If they are found in your stream, the best place to look for them is on the edges of white water at the head of a pool, or in runs and pocket water that connect the pools. Rainbows like lots of oxygen in their water, you say. Rainbows may like oxygen in their water but I don't think they live near the fastest currents for this reason. Rainbows also thrive in the Henry's Fork in Harriman State Park in Idaho, and most of this water is smooth, relatively slow, and without white water. You also find rainbows thriving in the spring creeks of Montana, and many of these have no white water.

The answer, I think, is food supply. Rainbows, unlike browns, seldom feed after dark, so they have to get all their energy during the day. They feed constantly. Rainbows also do more of their feeding on insects drifting in the currents, whereas browns may hold back until there is a heavy hatch, or until a foolish crayfish or minnow stumbles along. So rainbows will hold in water as fast as they can stand it, where they can maximize the amount of food that passes by their noses. Or they live in rich environments like spring creeks or tailwaters that overflow with food.

Browns, on the other hand, choose to live where the current is slower—not dead water unless there are a lot of insects on the water but farther from raging currents than rainbows. This is why rainbows and brown trout coexist in streams so well; their niches are segmented and one species seldom thrives at the expense of another.

A small stream near my house holds a healthy population of wild rainbows and browns. In the headwaters of the stream, the pools are so tiny they consist of little more than a head and a tail. Each tail holds one or two brown trout, which I usually spook with my first cast, and a rainbow on each side of the seam at the head of the pool, one of which I usually hook because the currents at the head of the pool hide my mistakes in presentation. At the other end of the scale, on the Madison you'll find the browns tucked in along the bank, wherever there is water over a foot deep and a log or bush for protection. The rainbows will be out in the seams on the edges of the fastest water. Jump over to the huge Yellowstone and the rainbows will be on the edges of the fast current, the browns on the margins of the eddies.

Even my friend Bob Bachman, who loves to play the iconoclast, has to admit "the niches of these species are neatly partitioned, like on the West Gallatin in Montana where I can tell with almost 100 percent certainty what species a trout will be as soon as it rises."

Unfortunately, the same happy equilibrium isn't true when you discover browns in the same waters as cutthroats and brook trout. And the result is usually in favor of the browns. While the rainbows frolic in the rapids, brook trout and cutthroats have similar niches to browns, and thus compete for the same spots. Brown trout are as adaptable a salmonid as they come. They grow quickly into a size that gives them an edge in disputes over places to live, and even the smaller ones appear to be more aggressive than brookies or cutthroats of the same size.

The Battenkill has many flat runs, shallow on one side and in the middle, and deep with overhanging brush on the other side. In the evening, when a spinner fall veils the water with insects, brown trout will be feeding on the deep, protected side, and the brookies, banished to water faster than they like and exposed to predators, will be on the shallow side. You can draw a line down the center of the river. It will separate the browns and brookies perfectly.

Several years ago, I found a trout rising all alone under a willow tree. Such a fish is invariably a brown of some size, as he will push other fish away. But there was something about the rise form that wasn't quite right. Still, I could tell by the depth of the *plunk* the trout made that it was one worth trying for. When I finally hooked the fish it went crazy, jumping and tearing around like a tarpon—I was using a #1-weight rod and the trout swam circles around me. When I finally got a look at him, it was an old male brook trout, just over fourteen inches long, one of the largest I've ever taken on the Battenkill. I caught that fish at least twice a year for the next three seasons, and he was always in the same place. He must have been a surly old cuss to hold off the local brown trout for three years.

Last season my old friend was gone, replaced by a sixteen-inch brown trout.

Territoriality

Some experts in trout behavior don't believe trout show true territoriality. When you think of an animal with a territory, something like a ruffed grouse drumming or an owl hooting comes to mind. They have a geographical territory with boundaries that are defended. Trout don't behave like this. A trout defends the site where he is feeding, the place he is resting his head at the moment, but if he moves to another rock, as one will often do in the course of a day, he will defend the place of current occupation with equal vigor.

Here's the way it usually works: A trout, let's call him a big, aggressive, dominant fish, is resting with his chin on a flat rock, feeding every so often. Another trout approaches from behind and off to one side of the dominant trout. The big fish shows no interest in the other one until the intruder gets even with his position or ahead of him. First, the dominant fish will flare his fins and stiffen his body—this is known as a lateral threat display. A sign like this from a larger fish is usually all it takes to drive away a subordinate.

If the smaller trout really wants to challenge the larger one, or if he is just dense, the dominant fish will show he means business by attacking the other, usually by nipping at fins, but on rare occasions one trout will grab another and bite, sometimes with serious results.

Displays will happen between members of the same species, and interchangeably among all species of trout and Atlantic salmon. It's interesting to note that a trout will not defend a position until he can see the intruder, so a trout behind another will invariably be subordinate to (and smaller than) the lead fish. The only time a smaller trout will be found ahead of a larger one in the same area will be when the smaller one is visually isolated from the bigger one by a rock or log.

Trout will form stable social orders called dominance hierarchies in a stream, centered around choice current lanes or pieces of cover. The biggest fish gets the best place, often the lead position in the current—which makes sense because if you're the largest, you want first crack at every piece of food that comes along. Let the little guys behind you mess with the midges and water striders, you only eat succulent mayflies.

What is this natural history lesson getting at? You just want to catch trout! There is a pragmatic reason for learning this—if you find a group of trout feeding, the lead fish is the most likely one to be the big slob. Conventional wisdom says that if you find a group of trout feeding, you carefully pick them off one by one, starting at the downstream fish. Wrong—at least if you like to catch big trout. Be greedy. You know the lead fish is the biggest, so carefully sneak around to the side of the pod of fish, and make your first cast to him. Sometimes you'll drop your line on the lower fish and they will dart upstream and spook the big one, but this only happens some of the time. If you start with the lower fish, often when you hook one of the little fellows he thrashes around and spooks the big one.

Other than at spawning time, wild trout in a stable population keep violence to the minimal level necessary to maintain a stable social order. They have enough trouble surviving without wasting energy on agonistic encounters. Even when large migratory trout enter a river full of smaller stream fish, there appears to be no disruption of daily life.

The Deschutes is a wide, powerful river, dam-controled and thus stable in flow and temperature, even though it runs through the desert. My friend Brian O'Keefe, who lives in Bend and has spent years fishing the Deschutes, says it is the most stable trout stream he has ever seen. Every year the nonmigratory race of redside rainbows is invaded by hordes of ocean-run steelhead, also rainbows but as different from a rainbow as a brown trout is from an Atlantic salmon. The stream fish run up to twenty inches, while the steelhead may be eight or nine pounds. Yet Brian says the trout are not affected at all by the steelhead, and seem to feed and behave the same as earlier in the season when there were no steelhead in the river.

"Are you sure the steelhead don't push the rainbows into the bank when they come through?" I asked him, thinking there must be some way their behavior was changed.

"No, in fact they'll sit side-by-side in a riffle, and I've caught them on consecutive casts," Brian said. Not convinced, I called Hilary Bates, another Deschutes fisherman and guide. Same answer.

If you want to see the disruption of a trout population, introduce a dozen or so hatchery fish into a pool filled to carrying capacity with wild trout. Bob Bachman did it in the population he observed on Spruce Creek, and he took movies that showed a striking example of trout behavior. You see a wild trout of eight or ten inches, lying in a stable, efficient pose on a flat rock. A hatchery trout six inches longer and weighing half a pound more than a wild fish bumbles over to it and first gets a shot of lateral threat display. It doesn't work. The smaller wild fish makes an outright attack again and again—finally driving the hatchery fish away. The next wild trout in line downstream repeats the performance until the hatchery trout gets pushed into a less desirable place in the pool, or it gets pushed downstream into another pool.

The process exhausts both the wild and the hatchery trout, and shows the folly of stocking hatchery trout in a healthy stream full of wild trout. It also shows you where to find hatchery trout if the river you're fishing is stocked—anywhere. Hatchery trout, at least recently stocked fish, don't

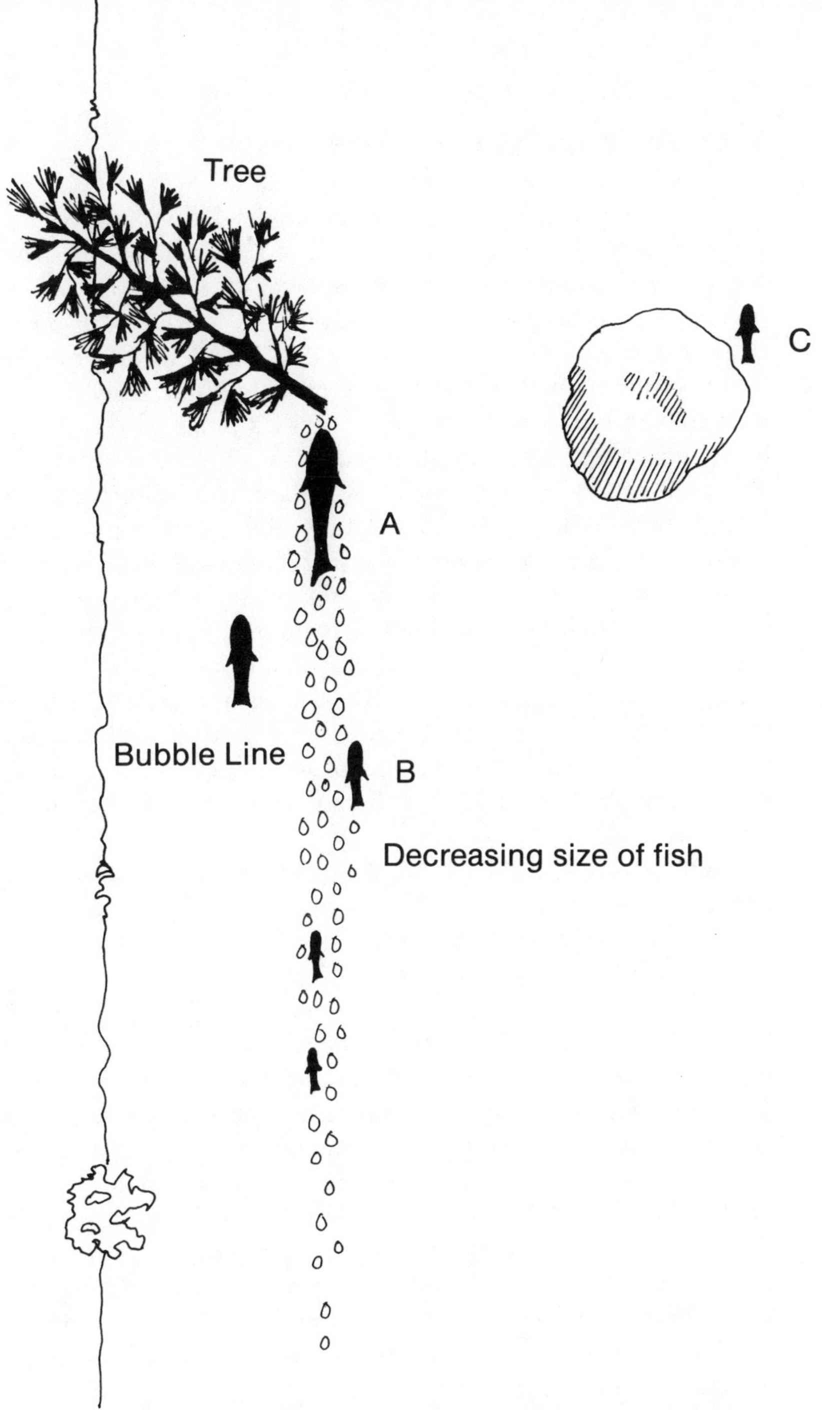

A hierarchy around a choice piece of streamside cover, in this case a sweeper. The big trout at A is the dominant fish and won't let smaller subordinates, B, feed in front of him. The small trout at C is visually isolated from the dominant fish and won't be attacked as long as he stays on the other side of the rock.

seem to be able to find efficient places to rest and feed as wild trout do. Thus they are unpredictable from our point of view. Even if trout were stocked months ago and have gotten acclimated to the stream, look in the logical places first but don't overlook the backwater over in the corner of the pool—a spot a chub would sneer at—or in fast water that would give a rainbow a muscle cramp.

Other Kinds of Fish

Do predator fish like bass, muskellunge, and pike have any effect on where trout will live in streams? Most of the evidence says they don't. In the English chalkstreams, riverkeepers hire local spin fishermen to remove big pike because the pike take a toll on the trout population. But most of the English streams are heavily stocked, and they are filled to well over the natural carrying capacity with dumb, slow hatchery fish—at least they're dumb and slow from a pike's point of view. A fox in a hen house never had a better situation.

I spent my teens on a limestone stream in upstate New York that was so rich in food it supported not only the finest population of fat wild brown trout I've ever seen but also a fair number of pike, smallmouth bass, and even carp. This is not unusual for a brown-trout stream. Not once in what amounted to about forty hours a week on the river did I ever see a bass or pike even show interest in a trout—nor did I ever see them occupy the same places in the pools. Bass and pike just cannot tolerate the currents a trout must have to get enough food. If rainbow trout and brown trout, as similar as they seem to us, have niches so far apart they seldom compete, imagine how dissimilar the niches of browns and northern pike must be.

Even suckers in the East and whitefish in the West don't compete with trout, because they usually live in the middle of deeper pools, whereas trout prefer the margins of the pools and places with more current. But suckers will sometimes fool you.

Non-trout fishers often come to you with tales of the "big school of trout we saw below Johnson's bridge." The best response is to thank them and ask them to pass that tip along to a fisherman you don't like. Trout may feed close to one another, but they don't live in schools on the bottom. Suckers and whitefish do. Another way to find a school of suckers is to do what the old books on nymphing told you to do—look for signs of "trout" flashing near the bottom when they are feeding on nymphs. With the exception of trout in spring creeks rooting for aquatic crustaceans, trout do not turn on their sides when they feed. Suckers turn sideways when they root under rocks for algae and small insects, and they do it all day long. I *have* seen a trout lying below a school of suckers, picking up insects the suckers dislodged, and this may be one reason the flashing trout theory has been perpetuated.

A lot of fishermen will have trouble accepting this but the next time you spot a fish feeding below the surface you *know* is a trout, look for flashes. Or if you see a fish flashing, get close enough to determine if it is a trout or a sucker.

Interactions with Man

Fishermen and boats can affect where trout hold in streams. Disturbances by man will drive the fish toward streamside cover or deep water, more so than if the population is infrequently disturbed. How does this

These people are obviously enjoying a sparkling day and a clear trout stream. They have as much right to use the river as the fishermen—but don't expect to find any decent trout feeding out in the open during the day.

happen? A trout is feeding out in the center of a pool, resting his head on a flat rock on the bottom of the river. A fisherman comes along and spooks the trout, sending the fish scurrying to the protection of a tangle of alders along the bank, ten feet from his feeding position in the center of the river. After a half hour of composing himself, the trout returns to his place in the center. Another fisherman stumbles along and once again sends the trout packing. Once this happens for a week or a month, the trout begins to feed right next to the alder tangle and returns to the center of the river only just before dark, and only if there is a heavy hatch of insects on the water.

The position near the tangle of alders may not afford the maximum in energy obtained vs. energy lost for the trout, but he feels more secure in that spot. Just how many boats or fishermen per day or hour does it take to affect a trout's behavior like this? No one knows—but we do know the more traffic a river receives, the closer to cover the trout will be at *all* times, not just when they are frightened.

Bob Bachman raises more than a few eyebrows at Trout Unlimited meetings when he says trout don't need overhead cover to feed; in fact, they prefer to be out in the open where they can see everything. Then he qualifies his statement by emphasizing that this is what he observed in Spruce Creek during his study period. The trout in his study area were not fished or boated over (except for an occasional poacher), so they were essentially an undisturbed population. This we can use as a baseline to learn where trout prefer to be if left alone—and where to look for trout in a river with low fishing pressure.

Contrast Spruce Creek with the AuSable in Michigan. The two rivers are ecologically similar. Both are characterized by smooth flow, wild trout, and a rich food supply. The AuSable has heavy canoe traffic in the spring and summer, and the trout, especially the larger ones, hold close to the sweepers lining the banks of the river. The big trout only come out into the center of the river during a heavy hatch.

Rusty Gates says the South Branch of the AuSable, which has the same current speeds as the main stem but far less canoe traffic, holds trout that feed and stay out in the middle of the river all the time.

It's not always a case of spooky trout moving from the middle of the river to the banks. Many times it is the reverse, especially if the water along the banks is shallow but the middle of the river is deep. When I fished the Madison for the first time, the guides in the fly shops kept telling me to be the first one up the bank in the morning because the big browns would be feeding right next to the bank until they were spooked out into the middle of the river for the day. Their advice was right on target. The one morning I got to the river early and trucked off upriver a mile so I could be sure there was no one ahead of me, I caught a lot of nice browns. The other times, when I got to the river in late morning or early afternoon the browns were toward the center of the river—harder to find and a lot tougher to hook.

9 Approach and Etiquette

Reading a stream is just as important for figuring out where to plant your foot as it is to decide where to cast a fly. Trout are shy. Their only defense against predators is to flee and hide. From my own experiences, and from watching other people work a stream, I am convinced that even the sneakiest fisherman spooks over 50 percent of the trout in a pool without even seeing them. Etiquette is entwined with approach because where other fishermen are is as important as where you think the trout are lying.

Trout Can See You

Trout never stop looking for threats that come from above the water. If they do they die. Contrary to popular literature, trout have not developed any adaptive mechanisms to protect them from man the predator. We haven't been stalking trout for long, at least not on the evolutionary time line. So we're lumped in the same category with kingfishers, herons, mergansers, ospreys, raccoon, and mink.

Trout can see out of the water, but they have two blind spots, without which we would catch even fewer trout. With eyes set on the sides of their heads, trout can see through a greater arc than humans, but there is a blind spot immediately behind them. The other blind spot is due not to anatomy but to the physical properties of water. Light striking the surface of the water at an angle of less than 10° is reflected and will not enter the water. Additionally, refraction gives a trout only a 94° window on the outside world, not a full 180°. For objects close to the surface of the water but outside of a trout's window, a trout has a blind spot all around him, even directly in front of him.

Because the same 94° window goes with a trout whether he is lying in shallow or deep water, a trout has more chance of seeing you when he is in deep water. The window is larger because the angle has more chance to expand before it is stopped by the surface, and the 10° angle that determines the blind spot has less chance to expand before it encounters your body.

I use what I call "the rule of six" to help me figure out how close I can get to a fish. Assuming the average trout you're stalking is about two feet deep in the water, multiply your height above the surface of the water times six—it will give you the distance at which you will be invisible to a trout lying under a smooth surface. If you're twenty-four feet away from a trout, you had better crouch so your profile is under the four-foot mark, and you should cast sidearmed. Not until we are thirty-six feet away can most of us stand erect without spooking a trout in clear water.

All else being equal, you can get closer to a trout by sneaking up behind him than you can by wading downstream. Many small-stream fishermen prefer the upstream approach to any other, because if you are wading downstream you have to stay at least 35 feet away from the fish. The only way you can get a fly to the trout is by casting directly downstream, because you don't have room to use any other kind of presentation in a stream that is only twenty feet wide.

I never thought about the long fly rod sticking above my head until I fished in England. The surface of an English chalkstream is placid; and trees have been cut to eliminate back-cast problems. Additionally, you always fish from a high bank, so anything that rises above your head is a sure alarm to the trout. One of the charming mannerisms of my host was the polite way he gently and repeatedly pushed my fly rod from the vertical to the horizontal. We seldom think of keeping our rod low when walking along the bank in this country.

Luckily, riffled water modifies how much trout can distinguish or even see above the surface. The rougher the surface of the water, the closer you can get to a trout. How close? In a fast riffle you can often fish directly across-stream to a trout that is only fifteen feet away. But be careful in pocket water; foam and riffles can hide the smooth slicks in between, and a trout can see you as easily from a smooth patch of pocket water as he can from the tail of a mirror-smooth pool.

You don't have to rely on riffled water to get closer to a trout than the rule of six allows. Even though a trout *can* see you, you might not make a threatening move. Many fly fishermen swear by camouflage garments and refuse to fish in the traditional tan vest. If you can blend into the brush along the river, they reason, the trout will mistake you for a piece of botany and not a hungry bird. Camouflage does not make you invincible. If you are fishing in a meadow stream and none of the bushes are over

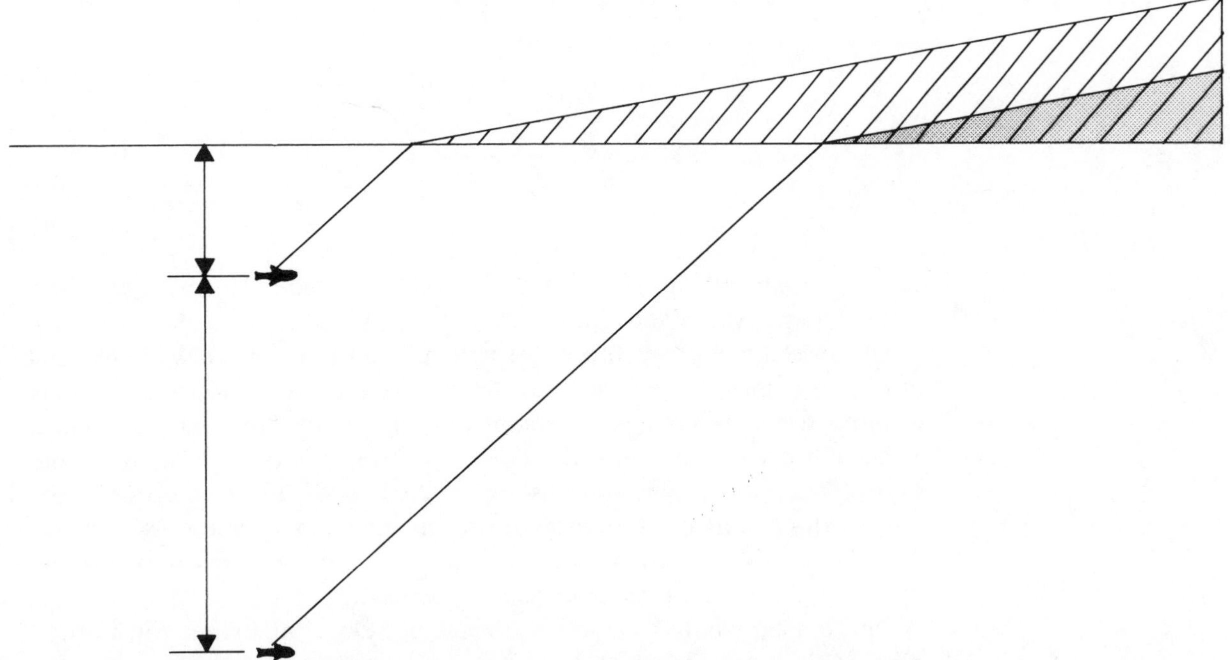

A trout carries his window with him. The trout in shallow water has a larger blind spot, so you should be able to get closer to him.

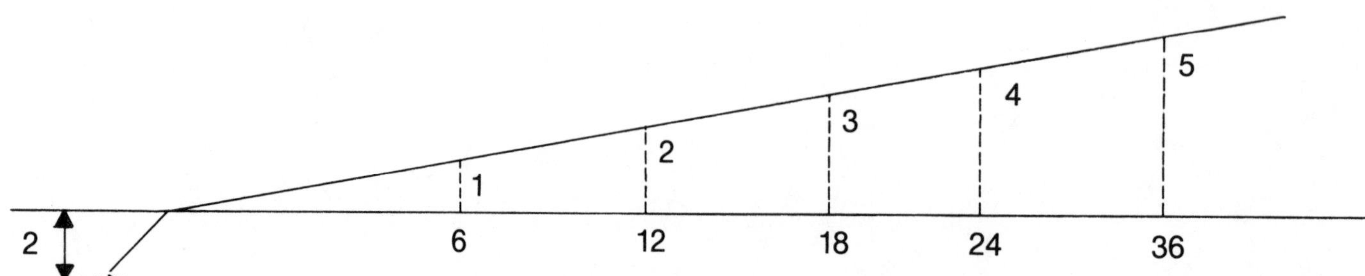

The "rule of 6," drawn to scale for a trout two feet under the surface. Numbers along the horizontal scale refer to distances away from the fish; numbers along the vertical lines are heights above the surface of the water below which things are relatively invisible to the fish.

two feet high, all the camo in the world is not going to make you less threatening if you stand up.

Shadows thrown over the water will spook a trout faster than anything else. Sometimes, though, the sun at your back is not a bad idea; trout are as blinded when looking at the sun as we are, and a trout has no eyelids. If he has to look right into the sun he will not be as likely to spot you. Many fishermen think trout fishing at high noon in clear water is too much of a challenge. I would rather try to approach a trout at noon than I would at six in the evening, because I can get the sun at my back without worrying about throwing a fifteen-foot shadow.

I have used windy days to my advantage. Once on a stream in California during unusually low and clear water, I spotted a group of brown trout rising at midday. The first time I tried for them, I couldn't even get within fifty feet of the feeding fish. The next day was so windy it bent the small trees along the river almost in half, and even though the surface of the stream wasn't riffled, I could get within twenty feet. All I had to do was creep up the side of the river, swaying instead of using jerky human movements.

Use common sense and imagination to keep yourself hidden from trout—or at least make yourself less threatening. A meadow stream that I fish in midsummer, when trout are skittish because the water is clear and thin, has a large herd of black-and-white cows that stumble along the banks and slosh into the water right next to where the trout are feeding.

Careful approach helped hook a nice trout. The fisherman stayed on the bank of this little meadow stream and avoided sending ripples into the water. He stayed behind the rising trout, and, to be on the safe side, kept his profile low by kneeling.

If you were careful, you could use these cows as camouflage. The trout here are used to seeing the cows in the river; if you blend in and move slowly, you won't frighten the fish.

The fish have gotten used to the cows, and don't miss a beat when they're rising and the cows are fewer than fifteen feet away. If I stand up on the bank I can't get within forty feet of the fish. But if I wear a white shirt and crouch so that I'm never above the level of a cow's back, and if I move as slowly as they do, I can get a lot closer to feeding fish. I've even thought of painting black spots on my shirt.

Trout can even get used to fishermen in the water; they can lose their fear of man if fishing pressure is so high that they *have* to feed when they can see you. Falling Springs Run in the limestone country of southern Pennsylvania looks much like the stream I mentioned above, but fishing pressure there is much higher, and the trout see fishermen twelve months a year, every day. You can almost stand on top of a feeding trout at Falling Springs, even though the trout are wild rainbows, the same species that I have to pretend I'm a cow to fool in the other stream.

Before you get into a river or stand on the bank to read the water, bear in mind the amount of fishing pressure on the river. You have to be more careful in a stream that is lightly fished.

Trout Can Hear and Feel You

In slow water, even if you stay directly behind a trout, in his blind spot, you can spook him from over sixty feet away. How? Trout can hear through an inner ear that has three chambers. Another sensory organ that warns them of movement in the water is the lateral line, a nerve running down the middle of the side of a fish that is sensitive to the slightest movement of water currents. Fishermen call the lateral line part of a trout's hearing mechanism, but biologists say it is closer to the way our sense of touch operates. It is so acute that large trout use it to pinpoint minnows and crayfish at night and in dirty water. Sounds travel better in water than in air, so don't underestimate the power of a trout's "hearing." I believe we warn more trout through their inner ears and lateral lines than by showing ourselves to them.

Ripples in a still pool will frighten trout; this is probably because of a combination of hearing, feeling, and seeing the ripples on the surface. In some rivers the care you take when stepping into the water makes the difference between an expert fisherman and a fruitless caster. The East Branch of the Delaware is a perfect example. Only a few miles from the heavily fished Beaverkill, it is never crowded. It cannot be approached with the same disregard that most fishermen give the Beaverkill; the fisherman used to the easy approach of the Beaverkill won't return to the East Branch after a single trip. You can step into the Beaverkill's riffled water and *then* start reading the water—the same trick on the East Branch will leave you casting over a lifeless pool. On the East Branch's tranquil football fields, you read the water by standing on the bank, sometimes for an hour or more, and only after you decide where the fish are, either by spotting rises or by looking at currents, can you plan your attack.

The dreaded waves can be avoided. (I'd be lying if I told you there is always a solution to a trout feeding in the middle of a dead-still pool.

I was so anxious to get my wife's eighty-seven-year-old grandmother into some rising trout that I didn't pay enough attention to the ripples we were making. We spooked the whole pool before she got a chance to cast over the fish. ***Photo by Margot Page.***

Some trout—happily—are uncatchable.) The easiest, and often the best, strategy is to move slowly. Watch the water in front of you—if waves emanate from you like the rings of Saturn you're moving too fast. One step every thirty seconds is not unusually slow for proper approach; if you think that sounds easy, time thirty seconds on your watch. Many fishermen don't have the patience. That's why the East Branch stays uncrowded.

Any object you can position between yourself and the fish will help break the waves. A log stretching across the river will stop the waves cold, and may let you get twenty feet closer than you could without the log. A fast riffle below the tail of a pool can be a gift, as the trout in tails of pools are so spooky that your first step into the tail will ruin the bottom half of the pool. Crouching or kneeling in the riffle, you can swing your leg like a chorus girl and the waves will never get to the slow water above.

On a piece of slow water on the King's River in California, a friend who had grown up nearby advised me to try for a group of rising fish from upstream. Stubbornly, I tried for them my way—from downstream—and despite careful wading pushed waves ahead of me that put all the fish down. Ed had tried for the same group of trout scores of times, and had found the only way he could get close enough to them was to work downstream slowly. Moving gently *with* the current causes less disturbance than pushing against it, if you are fishing a river that is wide enough for practical downstream casts. But you have to balance the downstream approach with the disadvantage of being right in a trout's line of sight.

Heavy footfalls on the bank should be avoided, especially on the kind of river with deep water along the banks and shallow gravel runs in the center. Trout hiding next to the bank can hear you coming. Stamping on the bank can make them bolt for cover when you are still sixty or more feet away, farther than most of us can deliver a fly with accuracy. Trout in streams that run through meadows are especially sensitive to vibrations along the bank. The ground is often soft and boggy, and this kind of soil transmits sounds more readily than rock or gravel banks. In rivers with wide gravel banks and extensive shallows sloping gradually into deep runs, the way you walk along the bank is not as critical.

Have you ever knocked two rocks together when swimming underwater? The sound is painful, even in a medium in which your ears were not designed to work. Imagine how threatening the sound of a rock rolling around on the bottom is to a trout, and think of how far underwater these sounds must travel. Be careful how you walk. Don't stumble into rocks. I used to wear felt-soled waders with aluminum studs in them, because I could almost walk up the side of a boulder. Then visions of the studs clicking like castanets on underwater stones made me retire them, at least in streams where the trout are uncommonly skittish.

Making Your Entry

Your demeanor on the bank, and where you make the first step into a pool, can be as important as the fly you choose. Plan a strategy. It doesn't have to rival Ike's D-Day scheme, but take a few minutes before you stride into the water. In fact, staying out of the water as much as possible is one approach you should consider. Don't walk into a pool at the easiest place to enter the water, wade upstream fifty feet to the place you want to fish, and then start casting. Instead, walk carefully along the bank and step into the water just upstream or downstream of where you intend to fish. The less fuss you make in the water, the fewer trout you will frighten.

In a river that has wide, gently sloping banks, where you are sure there aren't any trout near the shore, you can stride up the bank as carelessly as you wish. If the trout are sixty feet out in the middle of the river they aren't going to see or hear you. But along the kind of river where the deep pockets run along a wooded bank, or a meadow stream where the bank is high above the water, it's best to travel well away from the edge.

This is not the way to investigate a pool before you start to fish. Let's hope the fisherman has already fished through the pool and is just enjoying the view.

For instance, if you've parked at the upstream end of a series of pools that you want to fish upstream with a dry fly or weighted nymph, you have to walk down to the lower end of the water before you work back up. As you walk down, it's tempting to gawk over the bank to see if there are any trout rising. Don't. You are high above the water, thus visible even to a trout that is fifty feet away, and you are moving toward him; you're definitely a threat.

Instead, give the area you are going to fish a wide berth. Walk far enough away from the river that you cannot see the surface of the water.

Many pools and runs have a "good" side and a shallow side with no features and no cover or protection for a trout. Even though you may have to hike to get to the shallow side, to cross the river at a shallow riffle upstream or downstream, do it. It's easy to tell the deep side, even from a distance, as it will have bigger trees on it, the land will slope more steeply, or the main flow of the current will favor the deep side. It makes no sense to wade across a deep run, only to turn around and fish the water just above or below the crossing point. Yet fishermen do it every day.

You spook more trout than just those at the narrow band where you crossed the river because of a phenomenon called "ricochet" or "chain reaction." The trout you almost step on bolts for cover, and as he does so he passes another trout that also bolts. The second trout spooks a third and so on up the pool. In practice it doesn't always work that way, so take

This fisherman on the Willowemoc had to walk over a mile to enter the run from the shallow side. The result of a careful approach was a couple of nice brown trout from the far bank—where he would have entered the river if he was lazy.

heart. Otherwise we would never be able to approach trout. I have seen two or three trout streak past one that was feeding, and the riser kept on rising, unconcerned. From what I've observed a chain reaction happens about 50 percent of the time, but it is a factor you should address when you enter the water.

Never step into the lip at the downstream end of the tail of a pool without having watched it for a few minutes. You will spook unseen trout in this part of a pool, and they may bolt all the way to the head if the pool is only twenty feet long. Everyone does it, but there are better ways of handling the situation. One solution is to stay in the riffle below the tail and fish it as carefully and thoroughly as possible—better to spook trout by casting over them than by spoiling the water without even attempting a cast.

You don't want to fish the tail? Maybe the currents are too tricky, or you don't think there is a decent trout in the tail. Conventional wisdom shows the expert fisherman working every bit of water in a pool with precision and caution, but if you *know* there is a monster trout in the middle of the pool, why start at the tail and take the chance of initiating a

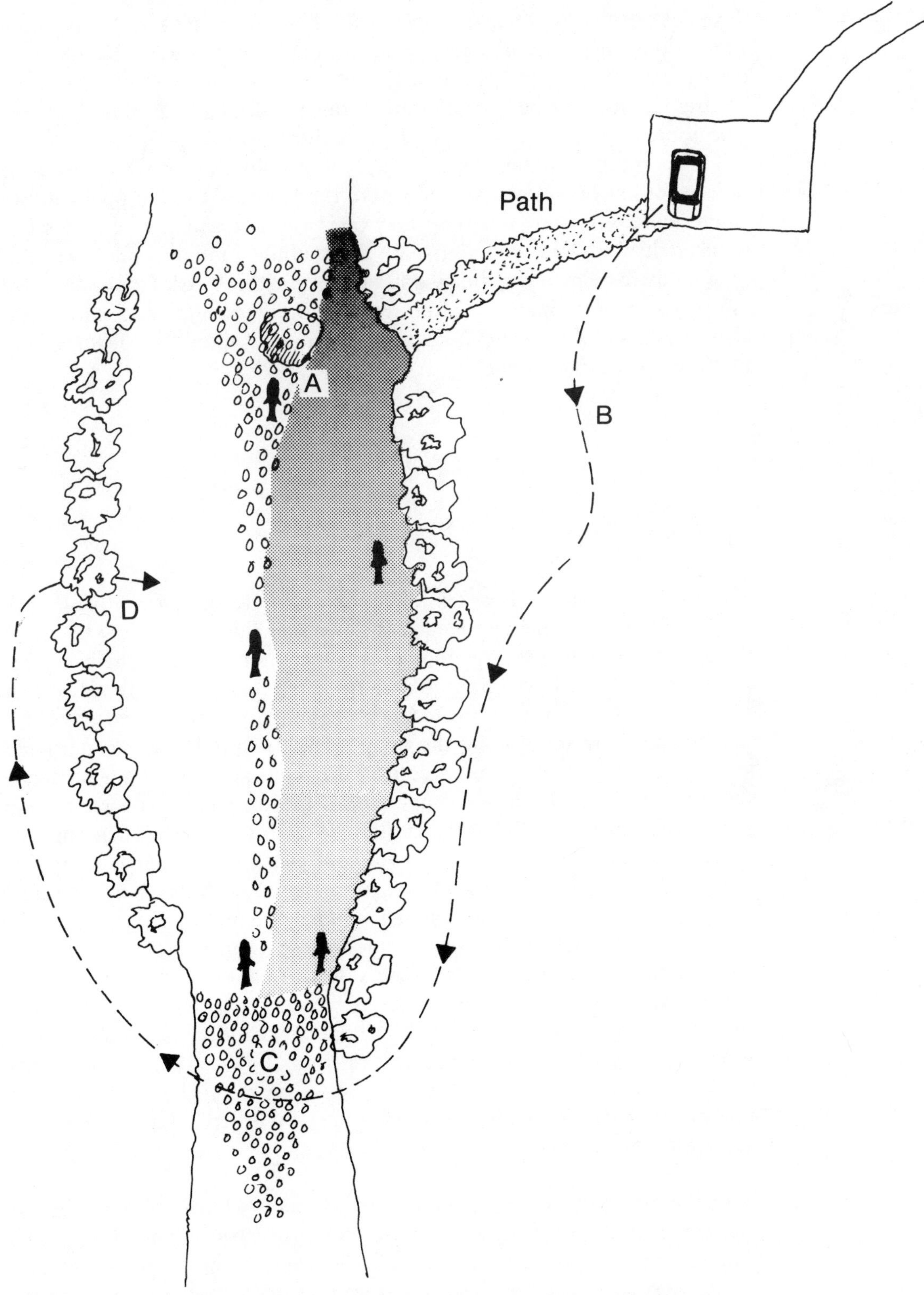

A wise approach to the trout at A: Walk well away from the deep bank, avoiding the easy path to the river (B). Cross in the shallow riffle below the tail of the pool (C). Enter in the middle of the pool on the shallow side, D, rather than the tail, to avoid spooking the trout in the tail up to the head and starting a chain reaction.

chain reaction? Here is a better idea: imagine where a trout in the tail of the pool can flee to when disturbed. Look for a big rock or log or some streamside brush. Then sneak along the bank until you are upstream of the trout's bolt-hole and slip into the water. Any trout in the tail, if they are frightened, will be cut off from a run up through the pool and will take the escape route between you and the big fish upstream.

This is the kind of sneaky thinking you should employ when you fish. Before you make a move, decide where the best trout in the pool will be. Then figure out where *any* trout may be. Last, determine where no adult trout could live—there is your path for wading through a pool. An old-time trout fisherman on the Esopus Creek in the Catskills always wore hip boots, even though the often-raging currents would seem to warrant chest waders. "Keeps me from wading where I should be fishing," he told me. Not a bad thought.

Etiquette

Cairns's Pool on the Beaverkill is a prototypical trout-stream pool, with a fast, riffly head, a moderate current down one side, and a slow tail. The deep bank is well over the tops of anyone's waders, and there are reported to be eight-pound brown trout along that bank. When I first started fishing the Beaverkill, it was a challenge in casting and presentation to catch the trout along the deep bank. In spring water conditions, you could not wade past the middle of the pool, and it took a good sixty-foot cast to reach the fish. Compounding the distance was a nasty drag problem because the fish were in slow water just inside of fast current. Fishing to those trout from their own bank was just not done. Everyone obeyed the rule and you could cast to rising trout all day long, because nobody could ever get close enough to spook them.

Then some bright fishermen decided those trout could be caught by crossing the river at the tail of Cairns's or upstream in Horse Brook Run, walking along the old railroad grade on the far bank, and along the bank (it's too deep to wade) and making short backhanded casts (unless you were left-handed). They caught nice trout. The problem was that Cairns's often has twenty or more fishermen working the bank, and the few guys who crept along the bank spoiled it for the others. There is something to be said for tradition.

In the first part of this chapter I talked about what to look for before stepping into a pool. I neglected to mention the most important object to look for—another fisherman. Not much is written about angling etiquette these days, and although there are more interesting topics sometimes we need to preach to one another. Ray Bergman's *Trout*, written in 1938 and the bible for generations of trout fishermen, is full of suggestions on how to minimize problems of use on our trout streams. We should be following the same code today.

Cairns's Pool early in the season, looking upstream from the tail.

An important right-of-way in Bergman's day was that of a fisherman working upstream. If two fishermen met while fishing, going in opposite directions, the one working upstream had the right of way, and the man or woman fishing downstream would get out of the river and walk around the other fisherman until he or she was a respectful distance away. Why the person working upstream? Someone has to have the right-of-way, and the person fishing upstream with a dry fly in those days was considered to have a handicap.

On today's trout streams, fishermen don't move around as much, preferring to work over a group of selectively feeding trout—at least in our more famous streams. Here, the rule should be that you allow another fisherman in a river as much space as conditions permit. If one fisherman is in a pool and there is not a soul in sight for several pools, don't wade into the pool the other person is fishing. You say you don't like the other pools as much? Tough. If there are fishermen in every pool, take the head of a pool if another person is in the tail. And if a pool is crowded, go elsewhere! Find a riffle or a piece of pocket water that doesn't get much attention—you might be pleasantly surprised.

If, while walking the bank, you come upon another fisherman, see which direction he's moving. If he moves upstream, wait until he is out of sight if possible, then get into the river and move in the opposite direction. If you can't tell which direction a fisherman is moving, ask. Often if he is working on a trout in the head he won't care if you fish the tail; a question like "Mind if I slip in at the tail?" is a welcome courtesy.

Time to find another pool, no matter how many big ones are rising here.

When you see another fisherman on the bank, smoking, tying knots, or staring at the water, he might be doing more than resting tired legs. If a good fish is spotted and worked over but not hooked, it's often good strategy to sit on the bank and regroup. Or some fish might be feeding and when you hook one, you disturb the water. Resting a pool or resting a fish are acceptable ways of tying up a pool, and if you see someone sitting on the bank you should ask if he is resting the water. If he *was* just resting his legs, he will tell you to "go ahead and fish through." If you aren't polite enough to ask, you may find out in an unpleasant verbal, sometimes even physical, manner.

Crossing the river, even if you are done fishing for the day and dog-tired, should be done in a thoughtful manner. Don't cross a pool where someone else is fishing—find a shallow riffle where you won't disturb water that someone else may want to fish later in the day.

I've often been working on feeding trout along a bank, only to have a friendly fisherman stop to gab, leaning over the bank, scaring every trout in the run. If you *have* to ask how someone is doing, stay well away from the bank—and shout!

Most of the world's trout streams are on private land. We are allowed to fish them through the courtesy of landowners, who are also the people who have to pull money out of their pockets to pay for riprapping a bank that is caving in—or for the barbed-wire fence that a fisherman cut, letting out the farmer's valuable animals. If land isn't plainly marked with public fishing signs, find the landowner and ask permission to trespass. Some of the finest spring creeks in Montana are private but available to anyone who is polite enough to ask nicely at the ranch house. As long as we police our own ranks we'll be able to enjoy some of this fine fishing.

Stream etiquette is a combination of common sense and the Golden Rule, and most of the etiquette problems today occur because few fishermen realize how shy a trout is, and how long he may stop feeding if he is frightened.

Respect these beautiful, wild, cautious animals—and while you're appreciating them, remember that in some rivers it may take a trout five years to grow to fifteen inches.

When you kill a large trout, how many years will it take to replace such a fish?

Selected Reading

ANDERSON, GARY. *Atlantic Salmon and the Fly Fisherman.* Doubleday Canada, Ltd., 1985. Detailed sections on where Atlantic salmon lie in rivers.

BERGMAN, RAY. *Trout.* Alfred A. Knopf, 1969. Though written in 1939, the technique, approach, and stream-reading sections are some of the best ever written.

BROOKS, CHARLES. *The Trout and the Stream.* Nick Lyons Books, 1974. Excellent stream-reading sections, written almost entirely for the streams in and around Yellowstone National Park, but valid for any big river.

CLARKE, BRIAN, AND JOHN GODDARD. *The Trout and the Fly.* Nick Lyons Books, 1980. Some of the best sections on how to find spring creek trout ever written. All studies were done on English chalkstreams but should have an application to weedy trout streams anywhere.

COMBS, TREY. *Steelhead Fly Fishing and Flies.* Salmon, Trout, Steelheader, 1976. The life history section in this book will give you a good idea on where to find ocean-run rainbows.

FALKUS, HUGH. *Salmon Fishing.* H. F. & G. Witherby, Ltd., 1984. An English title with some of the most innovative theories on where Atlantic salmon lie.

HILL, LES, AND GRAEME MARSHALL. *Stalking Trout.* Halcyon Press, 1985. A New Zealand title with excellent photographs of those incredibly clear New Zealand rivers, showing some real heart-pounders lying on the riverbed. A sight-fishing manual that will be invaluable for late-summer conditions anywhere in the world.

HUMPHREYS, JOE. *Joe Humphreys's Trout Tactics.* Stackpole, 1981. Helpful sections on small streams and on how to find a trout stream using a topo map and a thermometer.

HYNES, H. B. N. *The Ecology of Running Waters.* University of Toronto Press, 1972. A standard textbook of stream ecologists everywhere but accessible enough for the curious layman.

LEE, ART. *Fishing Dry Flies for Trout on Rivers and Streams.* Atheneum, 1982. Strong on tackle and tactics, with a short chapter on currents and stream features.

MARINARO, VINCENT. *In the Ring of the Rise.* Nick Lyons Books, 1976, 1987. A timeless study on the habits and habitat of spring creek trout.

NEEDHAM, PAUL. *Trout Streams.* Winchester Press, 1969. Though first written in 1938, this is still a helpful reference on the physical, chemical, and biological effects of the elements on trout and aquatic insects.

OVINGTON, RAY. *Tactics on Trout.* Alfred A. Knopf, 1969. A chatty discussion of various kinds of trout pools and how to fish them. Heavily oriented to the Catskills and upstate New York.

WULFF, LEE. *The Atlantic Salmon.* Nick Lyons Books, 1983. The grand master of Atlantic salmon fishing tells the secrets of a lifetime of finding fish.

WRIGHT, LEONARD M., JR. *The Ways of Trout.* Nick Lyons Books, 1985. The best study of an infertile freestone river ever done. Innovative theories on the effects of temperature on trout.

Index

Note: page numbers in italics refer to illustrations